CW00551671

PATHWAYS TO PROFESS. ᴐᴎᴀᴌᴉᴢᴍ IN EARLY CHILDHOOD EDUCATION AND CARE

Pathways to Professionalism in Early Childhood Education and Care is concerned with a growing interest from policy and research in the professionalisation of the early childhood workforce. Illustrated by in-depth case studies of innovative and sustainable pathways to professionalisation, it recognises the importance of a systemic approach to professionalisation across all levels of the early childhood system. The authors of this wide-ranging book share insights of professionalism from various European countries and suggest that professionalism in early childhood unfolds best in a 'competent system'.

This book considers a broad range of international issues including:

- Continuous professional support and quality
- Early childhood education and care staff with different qualifications in professional development processes
- How personal attitudes and the competence of educators are related to the wider system of competent teams, leadership, collaboration across services and competent governance
- From research to policy: the case of early childhood and care

Pathways to Professionalism in Early Childhood Education and Care is a crucial and fascinating read for professionals working in the sector and contributes to broadening views on what professionalism in early childhood can mean within a 'competent system'.

Michel Vandenbroeck is Professor at the Department of Social Work and Social Pedagogy at Ghent University, Belgium.

Mathias Urban is Professor of Early Childhood Studies and Director of the Early Childhood Research Centre (ECRC) at the University of Roehampton, London, UK.

Jan Peeters is the coordinator of the Centre for Innovation in the Early Years of the Department of Social Work and Social Pedagogy at Ghent University, Belgium.

EECERA
European Early Childhood
Education Research Association

Written in association with the European Early Childhood Education Research Association (EECERA), titles in this series will reflect the latest developments and most current research and practice in early childhood education on a global level. Feeding into and supporting the further development of the discipline as an exciting and urgent field of research and high academic endeavour, the series carries a particular focus on knowledge and reflection, which has huge relevance and topicality for those at the front line of decision making and professional practice.

Rather than following a linear approach of research to practice, this series offers a unique fusion of research, theoretical, conceptual and philosophical perspectives, values and ethics, and professional practice, which has been termed 'Ethical Praxis'.

Other titles published in association with the European Early Childhood Education Research Association (EECERA):

**Assessment and Evaluation for Transformation in
Early Childhood**
Júlia Formosinho and Christine Pascal
2016/PB: 978-1-138-90974-8

**Pathways to Professionalism in Early Childhood
Education and Care**
Michel Vandenbroeck, Mathias Urban and Jan Peeters
2016/PB: 978-1-138-91889-4

PATHWAYS TO PROFESSIONALISM IN EARLY CHILDHOOD EDUCATION AND CARE

*Edited by Michel Vandenbroeck,
Mathias Urban and Jan Peeters*

Routledge
Taylor & Francis Group

LONDON AND NEW YORK

First published 2016
by Routledge
2 Park Square, Milton Park, Abingdon, Oxon OX14 4RN

and by Routledge
711 Third Avenue, New York, NY 10017

Routledge is an imprint of the Taylor & Francis Group, an informa business

British Library Cataloguing in Publication Data
A catalogue record for this book is available from the British Library

Library of Congress Cataloging in Publication Data
Names: Vandenbroeck, Michel, editor. | Urban, Mathias, editor. | Peeters, J. (Jan), editor.
Title: Pathways to professionalism in early childhood education and care / edited by Michel Vandenbroeck, Mathias Urban and Jan Peeters.
Description: Abingdon, Oxon ; New York, NY : Routledge, 2016.
Identifiers: LCCN 2015041851| ISBN 9781138918887 (hardback) | ISBN 9781138918894 (pbk.) | ISBN 9781315688190 (e-book)
Subjects: LCSH: Early childhood teachers—Training of. | Child care workers—Training of. | Early childhood education—Study and teaching.
Classification: LCC LB1775.6 .P38 2016 | DDC 372.21—dc23
LC record available at http://lccn.loc.gov/2015041851

ISBN: 978-1-138-91888-7 (hbk)
ISBN: 978-1-138-91889-4 (pbk)
ISBN: 978-1-315-68819-0 (ebk)

Typeset in Bembo
by Swales & Willis Ltd, Exeter, Devon, UK

CONTENTS

CONTRIBUTORS

Steven Brandt is a lecturer at the Department of Social Work at the University College Ghent (Belgium) and a PhD student at the Department of Social Work and Social Pedagogy of Ghent University. He contributed to the CoRe study with an analysis on formal and informal learning activities in municipal child care centres in Ghent. He is currently doing a PhD on generational differences in aspects of professional identities in social work.

Claire Cameron is Deputy Director of the Thomas Coram Research Unit, Institute of Education University College London. With a professional background in social work, she began her research career in 1990 and has carried out many studies of the children's workforce with a particular interest in institutional and non-familial settings for children such as early childhood education and care, foster care and residential care. She was co-author of *Men in the Nursery* (1999, with Peter Moss and Charlie Owen); *Care Work in Europe: current understandings and future directions* (2006, with Peter Moss); and co-editor of *Social Pedagogy and Working with Children and Young People: where care and education meet* (2011, with Peter Moss). She has also written two volumes about the care and education of young people in public care: *Improving Access to Further and Higher Education for Young People in Public Care: European policy and practice* (2014, with Sonia Jackson) and *Educating Children and Young People in Care: learning placements and caring schools* (2015, with Graham Connelly and Sonia Jackson).

Chris De Kimpe has a professional background in social work. She worked for more than 30 years as a pedagogical coach for ECEC in the Pedagogical Centre of the city of Ghent. The main action topics in her work are diversity, parent support and social inclusion. She set up and processed new types of ECEC community centers and developed a competent system of pedagogical support for the workforce of municipal ECEC in Ghent. She participated in many European projects and European networks.

Since her retirement, she has been a member of the ISSA program committee and a collaborator of VBJK, Centre for Innovation in the Early Years.

Jytte Juul Jensen has been an associate professor and senior researcher at VIA, Pædagoguddannelsen Aarhus, Denmark. She has for many years been training pedagogues, the early years professionals in Denmark. Her latest research project is on Danish pedagogues' understandings of Danish practice in early childhood services. She has undertaken a wide range of cross-national work, including research, and given numerous lectures and papers at international conferences in many European countries, as well as outside Europe.

Arianna Lazzari is Research Fellow at the Department of Education of Bologna University. Starting her professional career as a pre-school teacher, she awarded the title of European PhD in Pedagogy in 2011, with a thesis on early years practitioners' professionalism. She has been involved in several research projects funded by the European Commission (*Study on competence requirements for staff in ECEC*, 2011; *ECEC in promoting educational attainment including social development of children from disadvantaged backgrounds and in fostering social inclusion*, 2012) and by Eurofound (*ECEC: working conditions, training and quality of services – A systematic review*). Her most recent work include the collaboration with Nora Milotay for the review of research evidence in support of the document *Proposal for principles of a Quality Framework for ECEC* (2014), a report of the working group on ECEC under the auspices of the European Commission.

Susanna Mayer is a developmental psychologist and researcher at the Institute of Cognitive Sciences and Technologies, National Research Council of Italy. She carries on research in the field of cognitive development and socialization processes in early childhood. In particular, she has studied interactions between young children during pretend play, their exploration of the physical properties of objects and communication between children and adults in ECEC contexts. She has investigated the role and functions of the coordinators of early childhood education and care services in Italy. She has participated in several studies on the needs of migrant families with young children.

Linda Miller is Emeritus Professor, Early Years at the Open University. She has worked both with and for young children throughout her professional life as a practitioner and teacher/practitioner educator. Her research interests centre on workforce policy and professionalization of the early years workforce in England where she has been involved in national consultations and government working parties. International work includes co-authoring an expert report for the University of Bremen on the training of early childhood teachers in England (published 2014) and leading on a collaborative project 'A Day in the Life of an Early Years Practitioner' resulting in the co-authored volume *Early Childhood Grows Up: towards a critical ecology of the profession* (Springer, 2012). Most recently she is Series Editor for the *Critical Issues in the Early Years* series (SAGE publications).

She serves on the editorial board of the *International Journal of Early Years Education* (Routledge).

Nóra Milotay is a policy officer at the European Commission, DG Education and Culture, School Policy Unit. After graduating from Eötvös Loránd University, Budapest, Nóra taught history and German at a secondary grammar school in Budapest for several years. She then received her PhD in modern European history at the University of Cambridge. After having worked on several aspects of school policy in Hungary and at the European Commission, since 2010, Nóra has been building up European policy cooperation within the field of early childhood education and care, which has gained an increasingly important role within the Europe 2020 Strategy. This work has involved an extensive cooperation with a wide range of European and international stakeholders, and leading and managing the thematic working group of Member States policy makers, researchers and practitioners on ECEC within the Open Method of Coordination. This group has prepared a proposal for a Quality Framework in ECEC in 2014. With a background in both research and practice, Nóra's focus is on the intersection of research, policy and practice. She has been an advisor on several international research projects on ECEC and member of the editorial board of the *International Journal of Childcare and Education Policy*, jointly edited by the Korean Institute for Childcare and Education and the National Institute for Early Education Research in the US. She has been a Salzburg Global Fellow in ECEC since 2015.

Myriam Mony is a consultant and trainer in social work and education in France and in transnational contexts, graduated with a master's in sociology and specialized in training and management in social and educational contexts. She worked as an educator and teacher for 15 years before working for 25 years as the director of training centers: first in ACEPP (National Coordination of 'Parental-*creche*' Network), later in ESSSE (Lyon, France), focusing on the bachelors training in social and care professions (initial and in-service training). She has been involved in transnational networks for the last 22 years (Diversity in Early Childhood Education and Training and the International Step by Step Association). She is also a voluntary worker in adoption contexts and in several NGOs. She authored the book *Entre laïcité et diversité quelles perspectives éducatives pour les jeunes enfants* and several other publications on social and cultural diversity and on working with parents in educational and adoption contexts.

Tullia Musatti was Research Director until 2012 at the Institute of Cognitive Sciences and Technologies, National Research Council of Italy, and since her retirement, has been Associate at the same Institute, where she coordinates the Human Development and Society Group and conducts research on young children's socialization and learning processes in the early years. Her main research topics are: peer interaction between young children, object exploration and pretend play, young children's daily life in early childhood education and care centers and at home, parents' perspectives on young children's care and education. She is the author of several books and articles in the field of early childhood development and education. She has participated in numerous working committees and projects to reorganize social and educational services in collaboration with Italian public administrations.

Jan Peeters is the Director of the Centre for Innovation in the Early Years of the Department of Social Work and Social Pedagogy, at Ghent University in Belgium. He obtained a PhD in pedagogy on a study on professionalism in Belgium, New Zealand, France, Denmark and the UK. He is a Board member of the International Step by Step Association (ISSA), an ECEC network of NGOs in 36 countries in Europe and Central Asia. He was a senior researcher in the 'Competences Requirements in Early Childhood Education and Care' (CoRe research, 2011), and the 'Study on the Effective Use of Early Childhood Education and Care in Preventing Early School Leaving' (2013–2014) both commissioned by the European Commission DG Education and Culture. He was the promoter of a systematic review on the impact of continuous professional development on children's outcomes, commissioned by Eurofound (2013–2015). Dr. Peeters has published several books and many scientific articles on professionalism, gender and diversity in ECEC.

Mariacristina Picchio holds a PhD in Education and is a researcher at the Institute of Cognitive Sciences and Technologies, National Research Council of Italy. Her main research topics are: evaluation of ECEC services, initial training of ECEC professionals and continuous professional development, and relationships between ECEC professionals and families with young children, with a specific focus on migrant parents and children. She contributed to designing a system of participatory evaluation of ECEC quality based on pedagogical documentation and participated in several action research projects in cooperation with Italian local governments. She was involved as teacher and supervisor in several initiatives of continuing professional development of ECEC practitioners and coordinators in many Italian regions and cities.

Ludmiła Rycielska is a social psychologist at the Institute of Educational Research (Warsaw). She teaches cross-cultural psychology, statistics and psychology of education. Ludmiła is a co-author of the book *School in Times of Internet*.

Marie Paule Thollon Behar holds a PhD in psychology and is Training Coordinator in ECEC in the Training Centre of Rockefeller Social and Health School, in Lyon, France. She teaches psychology to students in the University of Lyon 2. Her principal research aims are based on thinking in practice: analysis of practices and participative action-research. She is an expert for France in European research.

Mathias Urban is Professor of Early Childhood and Director of the Early Childhood Research Centre at the Froebel College, University of Roehampton, London. He works on questions of diversity and equality, social justice, evaluation and professionalism in working with young children, families and communities in diverse socio-cultural contexts. With Michel Vandenbroeck and Jan Peeters he coordinated of the European CoRe project ('Competence Requirements in Early Childhood Education and Care'). His current and recent projects include collaborative studies on early childhood professionalism in Colombia ('Sistemas Competentes para la Atención Integral a la Primera Infancia'), a 14-country study on 'Impacts of Privatisation of Early Childhood Education', and an international project on 'Governance and Leadership for Competent Systems in Early Childhood'. Mathias is an International Research Fellow with the Critical Childhood Public Policy Research Collaborative, a member of the PILIS research group (*Primera Infancia, Lenguaje e Inclusión Social*), Chair of the DECET network (Diversity in Early Childhood Education and Training), Vice President of the International Froebel Society (IFS), and a member of the AERA special interest group Critical Perspectives on Early Childhood Education.

Michel Vandenbroeck is Professor in Family Pedagogy at the Department of Social Work and Social Pedagogy of Ghent University, Belgium. His research domains include early childhood education and care, parent support and family policies, with a special focus on issues of diversity and processes of in- and exlcusion. He is a member of the editorial board of several scholarly journals, including the *European Early Childhood Education Research Journal* and has authored several books and articles in these domains. Together with Jan Peeters and Mathias Urban he coordinated the CoRe project.

Tatjana Vonta is Associate Professor, Senior Research Fellow and holds a PhD in pedagogical sciences. She was the Head of the Development Research Centre for Pedagogical Initiatives Step by Step, at the Educational Research Institute in Slovenia. She was included in many projects on the international level and as researcher or leader in national research projects. For 20 years she was involved in preparing future preschool teachers, students of master's and doctoral programs at the University of Primorska and in designing and implementing of the international master's degree program in leadership and early childhood development in Moscow. Although retired she continues her professional and research work as an external expert for the needs of the Educational Research Institute, International Step by Step Association and Open Society Foundation London.

Olaf Żylicz is Associate Professor of Psychology at Warsaw University of Technology. He taught developmental psychology and ethics at Warsaw School of Social Psychology and Humanities. Dr. Żylicz was a Polish coordinator of the international project on parental cultural models. He ran systematic evaluation of 'Where There Are No Preschools', an ECEC program for children from Polish rural areas. His record of publications includes the co-authored 'Teachers' Ethnotheories of the Ideal Student in Five Western Cultures' (*Comparative Education*) and 'Chidren's Activity and Their Meaning for Parents' (*Journal of Family Psychology*).

INTRODUCTION

*Michel Vandenbroeck, Jan Peeters, Mathias Urban
and Arianna Lazzari*

Looking at the history of early childhood education and care (ECEC) policies in the
European Union over the last two decades means looking at a story of a remark-
able success – or so it seems when we take as a measure of success the amount
of pertinent policy documents and related academic writing published during that
period. Aiming to transform itself into the world's 'most competitive and dynamic
knowledge-based economy' (European Council, 2000), Europe had clearly identified ECEC as a key policy area to realising an ambitious macro-political agenda.

The importance given to services for young children in European policy
(despite the fact that the EU has no powers to govern early childhood provision at Member State level) was mirrored, from early on, in the recognition
of the importance of the early childhood workforce. Quality for children, the
policies insist, depends on a highly skilled, motivated and valued workforce.
But it was not quite as clear what exactly characterises a productive relationship
between quality and qualifications, or what we mean by 'highly skilled'. The
Terms of Reference for the research project that led to this book – Competence
Requirements in ECEC – state that 'little is known about the relationship
between high quality ECEC services and the competences of the staff providing
it'. In consequence, the EU Commission identifies the need 'to work towards a
common understanding of the issue at European level'.

In CoRe, we endeavoured to do just that. We looked in detail at how professional
practice can be understood, and its development supported, in the highly complex
field of working with young children, families and communities. Considering the
diversity of a European Union consisting of 28 Member States, what approaches
have different countries taken – and what are the lessons that can be learnt from
practices developed by practitioners, training institutions and policy makers across
Europe? We explored conceptualisations of *competence* and professionalism in early
childhood, and we identified systemic conditions for developing, supporting and

maintaining competence at all levels of the early childhood system. The study consisted of a literature study, a survey on curricula for the different early years professions in 15 countries and a series of seven in-depth case studies on how these recent challenges are met in diverse contexts. Our approach, the methodology and findings, together with recommendation of action that we think should be taken at national and EU level, are documented in detail in the project reports (Urban et al., 2011a, 2011b) and other publications (Urban et al., 2012). Yet, the seven CoRe case studies have never been published before – they form the core of this book.

A short hindsight

In the years after the Second World War and even more so in the 1970s, ECEC slowly developed in most affluent countries. Since the 1980s, the economic crisis drew the attention of policy makers to the economic aspects of ECEC. As a result, a renewed attention to ECEC could be noticed, it focused on the role of ECEC for female employment and equal opportunities for men and women in the labour market (Moss, 1988). The idea that sufficient ECEC was a necessary condition for economic growth gained momentum in a context of economic downturn and falling birth rates. As a consequence, Member States were looking for possibilities to increase the number of ECEC places, while observing budgetary constraints, and thus were in search of cheap solutions. These were primarily sought in two directions: familiarisation and marketisation.

Familiarisation means the growing number of childcare places organised by mushrooming child-minders or family daycare providers. Indeed, in the 1980s many affluent countries stimulated home-based ECEC (Mooney & Statham, 2003). The idea was that, as these child-minders have low levels of education, they are at risk of unemployment and creating ECEC places with this workforce would therefore serve three goals: cheaper places, combating unemployment and facilitating female employment. This was the case in such diverse countries as Belgium, Hungary, Germany, New Zealand and many others (Mooney & Statham, 2003) and it was legitimated by a home as heaven ideology. Of course, as Moss (1988) rightly noted, whether it actually was cheaper depended on the pay, the conditions and the support given to these caregivers.

The second trend, privatisation, means that ECEC was commoditised as a good on the market and several regions (e.g. England, the Flemish Community of Belgium and the Netherlands, but also Taiwan, Hong Kong, some Canadian provinces and many others) have encouraged private initiatives, with less or no state funding to respond to the increasing need for childcare places. As staff costs represent the most important expense for private ECEC managers, it was obvious that the marketisation also reinforced the search for cheap labour force in ECEC (Moss, 2009; Osgood, 2006; Penn, forthcoming).

In sum, for several decades of the previous century, the political attention was predominantly focused on the *quantity* of ECEC. An eloquent example of this is the Lisbon Agreement (European Parliament, 2000) pleading for economic development in the EU and the subsequent Barcelona targets (European Parliament, 2002) setting quantitative goals for the numbers of ECEC places Member states should have on offer.

More recently, however, attention grew not only for the economic functions of ECEC, but also for its educational and social value. As Penn (2009) noted, while the economic function is merely concerned with the number of places, the educational and social functions also entail concerns about their *quality*. Conceptualisations of quality may considerably differ, according to different understandings of what constitutes the educational and social missions of ECEC (Dahlberg & Moss, 2005; Dahlberg, Moss & Pence, 1999; Penn, 2009). Nevertheless, there is overwhelming evidence that the competences of staff matters (Early et al., 2007). As a result, there have been several attempts to study professionalism in European ECEC (e.g. Cameron, Mooney & Moss, 2002; Oberhümer, Schreyer & Neuman, 2010).

In sum, while many Member States face a historical burden of having invested in a workforce with low qualifications, we now know that qualifications and competences matter. As a result, many nation states need to bridge the gap between the reality of the ECEC workforce and their ambition to invest in the best possible life for the next generation. This book presents different ways in which several nations are going about this endeavour.

People matter

The fact that more effort is needed to increase the quality of ECEC provision (Penn, 2009) and that competences of practitioners working with children, as well as ongoing support for them, are crucial in promoting ECEC quality (Children in Scotland, 2011) have progressively been acknowledged in the European research and policy debate. As stressed in the research overview conducted by Bennett and Moss within the cross-European programme 'Working for inclusion' (Bennett & Moss, 2011), the early years workforce is central to ECEC provision – as it accounts for the greater part of the total cost of early childhood services – and is the major factor affecting children's learning experiences and outcomes. In recent years, a growing consensus has emerged that the way ECEC staff are recruited, trained and treated is critical for the quality of early childhood services as well as for the educational success of all children.

Such a consensus is grounded on international research evidence showing that better educated staff are more likely to provide high-quality pedagogy and stimulating learning environments, which in turn, foster children's development leading to better learning outcomes (Munton et al., 2002). At the same time, research shows that staff competence is one of the most salient factors ensuring higher quality in educational interactions (Litjens & Taguma, 2010). Competent educators nurture children's development by creating rich and stimulating early learning environments, by intentionally sustaining shared thinking and logical reasoning in social interactions and by valuing children's initiatives for extending their learning opportunities (Pramling & Pramling, 2011; Sylva et al., 2004).

Despite the substantial evidence showing that staff qualifications matter, research also points out that qualifications *per se* are not sufficient to determine the quality of ECEC provision (OECD, 2012). The content of the training – as well as the methodologies adopted for its delivery – also play a crucial role in increasing the professional competence of educators. In this regard, research findings also show that continuous professional development initiatives ('in-service training') may be equally important as initial professional preparation ('pre-service training' leading to officially recognised qualifications), provided these are of sufficient length and intensity (Fukkink & Lont, 2007). A recent report on the importance of professional development, published by Eurofound, points out success factors for continuous professional development initiatives:

- a coherent pedagogical framework or learning curriculum that builds upon research and addresses local needs;
- the active involvement of practitioners in the process of improving educational practice enacted within their settings;
- a focus on practice-based learning taking place in constant dialogue with colleagues, parents and local communities;
- the provision of enabling working conditions, such as the availability of paid hours for non-contact time and the presence of a mentor or coach who facilitate practitioners' reflection in reference groups.

Professional development initiatives based on research-based enquiry or action-research can help staff reflect on their pedagogical practice and therefore contribute to its ongoing improvement. Many of the factors listed above are represented in the CoRe case studies in this book. We believe they can serve as a source of inspiration for developing more effective approaches for sustaining the professional growth of early childhood practitioners and the continuous improvement of their educational practice for the benefits of children, families and local communities.

CoRe: a European study

The political attention for not only quantity of ECEC but also its quality is reflected in several initiatives from the Directorate General for Education and Culture of the European Commission. It was clearly present in the 2011 statement on the importance of early childhood education (European Commission, 2011), as well as in a comprehensive study on competence requirements for the early childhood workforce, commissioned in 2010 to a consortium of the University of East London and Ghent University (Urban et al., 2011). The study consisted of a literature study, a survey on curricula for the different early years professions in 15 countries and a series of seven in-depth case studies on how these recent challenges are met in diverse contexts.

Projects like CoRe, as reported in this book, are exercises in interrogating complex contexts of public policy and professional practice. They require taking into consideration a multiplicity of perspectives, understandings and interests, all grounded in the diverse contexts of a large number of partners including, but never limited to, those of the members of the research team (Urban, 2012). The deliberate use of the term 'partner', instead of the ubiquitous 'stakeholder' with its managerial connotations (Thomas, 2012), is a first and necessary act of positioning undertaken by the research team driving the project. It recognises the agency of those connected to our project without pretending that CoRe is the only, or even main, focus of their interest. It is more likely that the 'stakes' they are 'holding' are in the local initiatives and projects presented in this book. Their legitimate interests come together with ours, the 'researchers', in a specific period of time in the CoRe project.

The complexity of the task of creating a better understanding of the 'competence requirements in early childhood education and care' in an entity as diverse as Europe led us to adopt a complex research strategy from the outset. We had to find ways to bring together very different aspects of situated knowledge and experience in one shared framework. The literature review enabled us to bring together and analyse condensed collective and disciplinary understandings of key concepts and terms underlying this project: profession, competence, quality, etc. The survey, carried out in 15 countries, enabled us to gather, interpret and systematise professional knowledge through the lens of a number of professional actors, each one with vast experience in ECEC practices in their respective country contexts. The two approaches (literature review, survey) opened windows into non-mainstream *conceptualisations* of professional practice, and into *informed interpretations* of how these translate into actual professional profiles, frameworks, regulations etc. in specific country contexts. However, in order to better understand *how things work* (Stake, 2010), we had to include a third approach into the CoRe research strategy.

The purpose of including a number of in-depth case studies into the project was to gain a deeper understanding of the background, the dynamics, the success factors and challenges of *specific* practices in their *specific* contexts. We were interested, in short, in the *thick of what is going on*, as Clifford Geertz might have put it (Geertz, 1973), and for *whom*, and *why*.

Case study work is, in the words of Robert Stake, 'the science of the particular' (Stake, 2010, p. 13). In other words, conducting case studies in a European research environment is certainly not the science of representation. Building a sample of cases studies (seven were selected and are now included as chapters in this book) is by definition a selective process that involves making informed choices about what to include in, and what to exclude from the overall study. Our choices for the CoRe case studies sample were framed by three parameters (Urban et al., 2012):

1. We wanted to include cases that are considered to be examples of *interesting practices of high quality* by experienced professionals, international experts and in international reports and literature;
2. We wanted each case to shine a light on a different approach to organising early childhood services and on different understandings of early childhood

professionalism across Europe and its variety of EC systems (e.g. *split* or *integrated* systems, *generic* or *specific* professions, different *levels of formal qualifications*, different professional *support systems*);

3. We wanted, as far as possible within the limitations of the project, to construct a geographically balanced sample, ensuring participation from countries in different regions of Europe.

What is the case? Framing the seven CoRe case studies

As mentioned above, case studies, by their very nature, are about specific practices and experiences, not about generalisation and representativeness. For the examples selected for the CoRe project, and the chapters in this book, this means that although the cases are situated in their specific regional contexts, our aim was not to study the countries or regions. Rather, we were interested in the particularities of the individual examples. Experiences made by colleagues at the Ecole Santé Social Sud-Est (ESSSE) in Lyon may be situated in France – and some understanding of the French ECEC context is needed in order to make sense of them – but they are by no means representative of the French early childhood system in general.

CoRe case studies were conducted by local experts and project partners (the authors of the chapters compiled in this book) according to a briefing document provided by the CoRe research team. The document asked the authors to provide a *thick description* of the case, drawing on information gathered in ways they thought most appropriate for their example, including document analyses, focus group discussions, conversations, own observations etc. We asked all authors to provide some contextual information (e.g. relevant local policies, regulations) and a discussion of the understanding of professional knowledge underpinning their particular case. More specifically, we asked the authors to address the following aspects:

- Professional knowledge, theory and practice: how are they understood, what is seen as relevant (and why), who takes part in the co-construction of professional knowledge?
- Critical reflection and transformative practice: who are the actors in the specific case? How are practitioners, children, families and communities involved in the specific practices?
- Structural aspects of professional practice and their implications: e.g. job mobility, diversity and equality, gender, pay, autonomy, time and resources.

Given the diversity of the cases it was clear that not all case studies would address these aspects in this particular order or in clear distinction. We expected overlap and blurring of boundaries to be the norm rather than the exception. Authors were strongly encouraged not to press an interesting example into shape as to fit the questions. This was a two-pronged approach that allowed for the greatest possible amount of freedom for the authors while at the same time creating a structural equivalence (Burt, 1982) that allowed a shared analysis across complex documented experiences. The methodology of free standing but related case studies builds on approaches taken by previous research projects, in particular the Strategies for Change project (Urban, 2007) and the Day in the Life of an Early Years Practitioner project (Miller et al., 2012). Such an approach requires a huge amount of *trust* in the professional judgement of partners and a willingness by the research team to follow David Winnicott's trust in young mothers: 'To begin with, you will be relieved to know that I am not going to tell you what to do' (Winnicott, 1987, p. 15).

The seven case studies conducted for CoRe

The seven case studies conducted for CoRe are:

* The Danish Pedagogue Education: principles, understandings and transformations of a generalist approach to professionalism – Paedagoguddanelsen JYDSK, VIA University College, Denmark.
* A qualifying training at BA level of *Éducateurs Jeunes Enfants* (EJE) for early years workers with low qualifications – Ecole Santé Social Sud-Est, Lyon, France.
* Origins and evolution of professionalism in the context of municipal ECEC institutions – City of Pistoia, Italy.
* Pedagogical Guidance as pathway to professionalisation – City of Ghent, Belgium.
* Inter-professional collaboration in preschool and primary school contexts – Slovenia.
* Professional and competence development in the context of the 'Where There Are No Preschools' (WTANP) project – Poland.
* The Integrated Qualifications Framework and the Early Years Professional Status: a shift towards a graduate led workforce – England.

Reaching beyond the mainstream

One of the unique features of the CoRe research project was that it could benefit from the input of scholars from many different countries and therefore from literature beyond the mainstream. Indeed, mainstream literature is published merely in English and the dominance of English in academic literature inevitably also entails an impoverishment, as it either silences some fields of study, or translates them into what makes sense for an English language audience. In both cases something of the plurality of perspectives risks getting lost. In fact, the diversity of welfare states, ECEC and training systems in Europe over time has generated a great variety of professional development approaches across countries (Oberhümer, 2012). It has been documented, however, that such richness of approaches is not fully and equally represented in English language literature, due to the fact that research studies carried out in this field – ECEC institutions and their workforce – tend to be closely linked to countries' welfare traditions and educational cultures (Eurofound, 2015). As a consequence, impact studies evaluating the effectiveness of designed training programmes tend to be over-represented in English language literature, dominated by studies from the US, Australia and the UK where the investment in ECEC has been traditionally justified by economic productivity arguments. On the contrary, studies exploring broader social pedagogical approaches and participatory methods to practitioners' ongoing professionalisation are more often found in academic literature published in national languages, within those countries where ECEC has been, since its inception, considered as a public good within a 'children's right' rationale (see Penn, 2009 for a more in-depth analysis of political and welfare rationales).

The English language literature reviewed in the CoRe study highlighted that the relationship between ECEC quality and staff qualification is far from being causal but rather depends on the interaction of multiple factors, such as:

- the content of training programmes (curriculum design);
- the delivery of training programmes (the strategies that are used to combine theory and practice);
- the contextual conditions provided by the settings where training interventions take place (e.g. availability of non-contact time, team work, or supervision).

From this review, it also emerged that such factors are still largely unexplored in Anglo-American literature. Therefore, the scope of the review has been widened in order to include literature published in other European languages (French, Italian, Danish, Croatian and Dutch, as these were the languages spoken in the research team), offering interesting insights for re-framing the concept of competence within the broader study.

The Italian literature sheds light on the systemic conditions that are necessary for linking quality with professional competences. The issue of early childhood professionalism in Italy has been explored in relation to ECEC quality within a specific strand of literature that originated during the 1990s in accordance with an international trend and with reference to the work of the European Commission Childcare Network. During this period, several regional and local governments supported the experiences of participatory evaluation of early childhood institutions (*nidi*), which were carried out together by policy makers, local administrators, pedagogical coordinators and university researchers, and which involved practitioners and families (Barberi et al., 2002). The aim of these studies was not only to promote quality within ECEC services but also to reflect, at the institutional level, on the concept of quality as defined in relation to the needs expressed by all the actors involved. In this perspective, quality was defined as 'a democratic process of negotiating aims and goals by enhancing public debate on educational issues' and the process of participatory quality evaluation was conceived in formative terms (Bondioli & Ghedini, 2000). Participatory educational evaluation, in this sense, is seen as a hermeneutical process that fosters competence development by promoting a critical problematisation of practitioners' educational actions: the result of this ongoing process is the collective production of exchangeable professional knowledge (Musatti et al.,

2010). Therefore, in the Italian context, collegiality (*collegialità*) is a key feature of ECEC work, nurturing professionalism through practitioners' mutual commitment ('educational co-responsibility') towards the achievement of common purposes made explicit in the pedagogical project of the early childhood service. This collegial approach to staff professionalisation is rooted in the experiences of community involvement and parents' participation, matured in the context of municipal services in Northern and Central Italy over the last 40 years. It contributed to shape the role of early childhood practitioners in relation to the needs of children, families and local communities within which and for which early childhood services were conceived (Galardini & Giovannini, 2001).

In Croatian literature too, issues of professional competence and the professional development of early childhood practitioners are discussed within a systemic approach to the quality of educational institutions. Within this strand of literature, educational quality is not conceived as the result of individual practitioners' interventions, but it is rather considered a feature of the entire context of the institution, of which practitioners are an integral part and which practitioners can change according to their degree of understanding. Within this approach, it is argued that enhancing practitioners' understandings of the institutional contexts in which they are operating enables them to shape new beliefs for the development of educational practices aimed at improving the quality of the institutions (Žogla, 2008). In this sense, a crucial role is played by professional development that should be carried out within institutions themselves and that should be focusing on joint action-research (Slunjski, 2008), self-evaluation (Ljubetid, 2008) and collective reflectivity on educational practices generating new theoretical knowledge (Šagud, 2008). In this context, practitioners' professional development is conceptualised as a continuous process that – being subject to review and change – raises the level of practitioners' pedagogical competence. Within this strand of literature, the role of practitioners is currently being redefined within a shifting paradigm that conceives ECEC institutions as democratic learning communities promoting children's development from a rights-based perspective, which is framed by the UN Convention on the Right of the Child (Milanovid et al., 2000). Within this shift of paradigm, practitioners' professionalism is grounded on ethically responsible educational practices that are inextricably linked to the external social context. In this sense, the introduction of open communication with equal rights for every participant in the educational process, the enhancement of a culture of quality, and the increased consciousness for responsibility in a collegial and individual manner become essential elements of ethically responsible practices (Krstovid & Čepid, 2005).

The Danish interpretation of professionalism is closely connected to the view of the 'competent child' (Brembeck et al., 2004). Therefore, early childhood teaching is not seen as a specific activity, but it is rather perceived as a side issue (Jensen & Langsted, 2004). In a child-oriented approach to care, the concern exists that the nursery schools afford children so much freedom that learning and development may be compromised in some way. This concern led to discussion and to the reforming of the 'Nordic model' during the last decades of the twentieth century (Broström, 2006). In the law of 1964 instituting ECEC services in Denmark, there were no guidelines for the pedagogical content of the work of the 'pedagogue'; only some general aims and educational principles were described (Broström, 2006). Instead, in 2004 – following PISA results showing that Danish children's learning was at a low level – a curriculum was introduced for young children. Even though the curriculum is very open and reflects the nursery school tradition, many Danish pedagogues and researchers view the curriculum act as a problematic step towards more bureaucratic state regulation and as an adjustment to schooling (Broström, 2006). The professional organisation of pedagogues, BUPL, reacted to this challenge by making the pedagogic vision of the pedagogue more explicit by initiating a discussion on the interpretation of professionalism (BUPL, 2006). The professional expertise of the pedagogues is based on personal competences and on an awareness of one's own norms and values. It encompasses both theoretical and practical knowledge of the development of children, of play and of friendship. The Danish pedagogues state that their work can be described as multidimensional: providing care, socialisation of the community, '*Bildung*' for citizenship and democracy and learning through the development of individual skills (BUPL, 2006). For this reason, professional preparation of prospective pedagogues cannot only be concerned with theoretical learning within higher education institutions or with the mastery of practical skills in the workplace (Bayer, 2001). Instead, given the multidimensional professionalism that characterise pedagogues, initial professional preparation and competence development is seen as a recursive interplay of theory and practice that takes place along a continuum from the college to the workplace and from the workplace to the college (Bayer, 2001).

Along the same line, within the French context, the method of *analyse des pratiques* for professional development of social and educational professions was elaborated by the Parisian *Centre de Recherche sur la Formation*. By considering professionalisation as an infinite process of competence transformation in relation to a process of transformation of educational practice, the objective of this method is to reflect on professional practice from a theoretical framework (Barbier, 2006; Wittorski, 2005). This professionalisation process is steered and supported through the analysis of the students' and professionals' practical experiences, which first takes place on an individual basis and then in groups (Meunier, 2004). In the French context, this methodology is adopted either in the training courses for *Educateurs Jeunes Enfants* and in team-based professional development initiatives within early childhood services (Fablet, 2004). In fact, the method of *analyse des pratiques* does not solely aim at the acquisition of knowledge, but also at the production of knowledge starting from concrete situations (Meunier, 2004). In the first year, via this analysis of internship experiences, the foundations are laid for a personal track towards professionalism. In the second and third years, the situations that the students experience and that have raised questions are discussed in the group. Using this approach, Meunier (2004) seeks to develop new competences among the students, so that it then becomes possible for them – later, as professionals – to anticipate unforeseen pedagogic situations. Therefore, the *analyse des pratiques* is a method intending to elicit more questions than answers and this in the context of critical analysis and co-operation (Favre, 2004). By discussing the situations in the group – and by seeking solutions collectively – the *analyse des pratiques* contributes to the creation of a theoretical basis for pedagogic actions. With this position, Favre concurs with Dahlberg and Moss (2005) advocating 'minor politics', by which professionals, children and parents together create a new type of knowledge.

In the Netherlands and Belgium there is a tradition of pedagogical coaching to increase the level of professionalism for low qualified childcare workers. Such experiments started in the 1980s and were supported by grants from the Bernard van Leer Foundation. In Flanders, the first experiments were set up in the 1990s in Ghent (Peeters, 1993, see the chapter on the Ghent case study in this book) in the Netherlands (Van Keulen & Del Barrio, 2010) and the French-speaking part of Belgium (Pirard, 2005). In the Flemish experiments, the professionalisation process is considered as a social practice and as a result of complex interactions between social evolutions (e.g. the growing diversity of families), policy measures (e.g. new legislation) and new scientific insights. The pedagogical counselling or coaching projects in Belgium and the Netherlands focus on practitioners as active actors in their own professionalisation process, which has a motivating effect on the learners (Peeters & Vandenbroeck, 2011; Van Keulen & Del Barrio, 2010).

The review of non-English-language literature carried out within the CoRe study lead to the conclusion that a narrow conceptualisation of competence as a set of predefined knowledge, skills and attitudes universally applicable is not appropriate in the ECEC field. Rather, professional competences in the ECEC field need to be conceptualised within a multidimensional framework – which encompass both individual and collective components – and understood as a process that constantly evolves in socio-cultural contexts. In sum, rather than discussing staff competences, we need to discuss competent *systems*, consisting of four levels of competences. The first level is the level of individual practitioners and at this level the study advocates for combinations of pre-service training and sustained in-service training. Equally important is the second level of team competences, including for instance paid hours away from the children to make in-service training sustainable. The third level is the level of inter-institutional competences, favouring the collaboration between local early years provision with other social, educational and cultural institutions. And finally there is the crucial level of governance competences regarding vision, finance and monitoring. For each of these levels, the CoRe study formulated examples of competences about knowledge, practices and values. While the conclusions and recommendations of the study have been disseminated, the case studies, generating thick and rich insights, have remained unpublished so far. The case studies presented in the following chapters shed light on how ECEC practitioners' competences can be fostered through the diversity of approaches and methods elaborated within EU member states' pedagogical traditions.

References

Barberi, P., Bondioli, A., Galardini, A., Mantovani, S. & Perini, F. (2002). *Linee guida per la qualità del servizio asilo nido nella provincia di Trento.* Trento: Giunta della Provincia Autonoma.

Barbier, J. M. (2006). Problématique identitaire et engagement des sujets dans les activités. In J. M. Barbier, E. Bourgeois, G. De Villiers & M. Kaddouri (Eds.), *Constructions identitaires et mobilisation des sujets en formation.* Paris: L'Harmattan, pp. 15–64.

Bayer, M. (2001). *Praktikkens skjulte læreplan: praktikuddannelse – empirisk undersøgt i pædagoguddannelsen.* Copenhagen: Danmarks Pædagogiske Universitets Forlag.

Bennett, J. & Moss, P. (2011). *Working for inclusion: how early childhood education and care and its workforce can help Europe's youngest citizens.* Edinburgh: Children in Scotland. Retrieved from: www.childreninscotland.org.uk/wfi/.

Bondioli, A. & Ghedini, P. O. (2000). *La qualità negoziata: gli indicatori per i nidi della Regione Emilia-Romagna.* Bergamo: Edizioni Junior.

Brembeck, H., Johansson, B. & Kampmann, J. (2004). *Beyond the competent child: exploring contemporary childhoods in the Nordic welfare societies.* Roskilde: Roskilde University Press.

Broström, S. (2006). Curriculum in preschool. *International Journal of Early Childhood*, 38(1), 65–76.

BUPL (2006). *The work of the pedagogue: roles and tasks.* Copenhagen: BUPL.

Burt, R. S. (1982). *Toward a structural theory of action: network models of social structure, perception, and action.* New York and London: Academic Press.

Cameron, C., Mooney, A. & Moss, P. (2002). The child care workforce: current conditions and future directions. *Critical Social Policy*, 22(4), 572–595.

César, A., Dethier, A., François, N., Legrand, A. & Pirard, F. (2012). *Recherche-Action 114: formations initiales dans le champ de l'accueil de l'enfance (0–12 ans).* Liège: Université de Liège.

Dahlberg, G. & Moss, P. (2005). *Ethics and politics in early childhood education.* London: Routledge.

Dahlberg, G., Moss, P. & Pence, A. (1999). *Beyond quality in early childhood education.* London: Falmer.

Early, D., Maxwell, K., Burchinal, M., Bender, R., Ebanks, C., Henry, G. & Vandergrift, N. (2007). Teachers' education, classroom quality, and young children's academic skills: results from seven studies of preschool programs. *Child Development*, 78(2), 558–580.

Eurofound (2015). *Working conditions, training of early childhood care workers and quality of services: a systematic review.* Luxembourg: Publications Office of the European Union.

European Commission (2011). *Early childhood education and care: providing all our children with the best start for the world of tomorrow.* Brussels: European Commission.

European Parliament (2000). *Lisbon European Council 23 and 24 March 2000: presidency conclusions.* Brussels: European Parliament and Council.

European Parliament (2002). *Presidency conclusions: Barcelona European Council – 16 March 2002.* Brussels: European Parliament and Council.

Fablet, D. (Ed.) (2004). *Professionnel(le)s de la petite enfance et analyse de pratiques.* Paris: L'Harmattan.

Favre, D. (2004). Quelques réflexions de formateur sur l'analyse des pratiques professionnelles en secteur petite enfance. In D. Fablet (Ed.), *Professionnel(le)s de la petite enfance et analyse de pratiques.* Paris: L'Harmattan, pp. 17–38.

Fukkink, R. & Lont, A. (2007). Does training matter? Meta-analysis and review of caregiver training studies. *Early Childhood Research Quarterly*, 22(3), 294–311.

Galardini, A. & Giovannini, D. (2001) Pistoia: creating a dynamic, open system to serve children, families and community. In L. Gandini & C. Pope Edwards (Eds.), *Bambini: Italian experiences of infant and toddler care*. New York: Teachers' College Press, pp. 89–105.

Geertz, C. (1993). *The interpretation of cultures: selected essays*. London: Fontana.

Jensen, J. & Langsted, O. (2004). Dänemark: Pädagogische Qualität ohne nationales Curriculum. In W. Fthenakis & P. Oberhümer (Eds.), *Frühpädagogik international: bildungsqualität im blickpunkt*. Wiesbaden: Verlag für Sozialwissenschaften, pp. 119–208.

Krstovid, J. & Čepid, R. (2005). Development trends in teacher training within the context of lifelong learning: the experience of Croatia In Š. Švec & M. Potočárová (Eds.), *Razvoj študijného a vedného odboru pedagogika na slovensku*. Bratislava: Univerzita Komenského, pp. 119–125.

Litjens, I. & Taguma, M. (2010). *Revised literature overview for the 7th meeting of the OECD network on early childhood education and care*. Paris: OECD. Retrived from www.oecd.org/officialdocuments/publicdisplaydocumentpdf/?cote=EDU/EDPC/ECEC%282010%293/REV1%20&doclanguage=en.

Ljubetid, M. (2008). Teachers' professional development: qualifying for quality self evaluation and educational practice reflection. In I. Žogla (Ed.), *Teacher of the 21st century: quality education for quality teaching*. Riga: University of Latvia Press, pp. 597–604.

Meunier, Y. (2004). L'analyse des pratiques en formation initiales d'éducateur de jeunes enfants. In D. Fablet (Ed.), *Professionnel(le)s de la petite enfance et analyse de pratiques*. Paris: L'Harmattan, pp. 111–132.

Milanovid, M., Stričevid, I., Maleš, D. & Sekulid-Majurec, A. (2000). *Early childhood care and development in the Republic of Croatia*. Zagreb: Targa.

Miller, L., Dalli, C. & Urban, M. (Eds.) (2012). *Early childhood grows up: towards a critical ecology of the profession*. Dordrecht and London: Springer.

Mooney, A. & Statham, J. (2003). *Family day care: international perspectives on policy, practice and quality*. London: Jessica Kingsley Publishers.

Moss, P. (1988). *Child care and equal opportunity: consolidated report to the European Commission*. Brussels: European Commission Network on Child Care and Other Measures to Reconcile Employment and Family Responsibilities.

Moss, P. (2009). *There are alternatives: markets and democratic experimentalism in early childhood education and care* (Vol. 53). The Hague: Bernard Van Leer Foundation.

Musatti, T., Picchio, M. & Di Giandomenico, I. (2010). *Valutare in un sistema integrato, in AAVV: la qualità dei servizi per l'infanzia nella società globale*. Bergamo: Edizioni Junior, pp. 131–136.

NESSE (2009). *Early childhood education and care: key lessons from research for policymakers*. Brussels: European Commission. Retrieved from: http://ec.europa.eu/education/news/news1697_en.htm.

Munton, T., Mooney, A., Moss, P., Petrie, P., Clark, A., Woolner, J., et al. (2002). *Research on ratios, group size and staff qualifications and training in early years and childcare settings*. London: University of London and the Department for Education and Skills.

Oberhümer, P. (2012). *Fort- und Weiterbildung frühpädagogischer Fachkräfte im europäischen Vergleich* [The education and training of the early years workforce in European comparison]. Munich: Deutsches Jugendinstitut. Retrieved from: www.weiterbildungsinitiative.de/uploads/media/Studie_Oberhümer.pdf.

Oberhümer, P., Schreyer, I. & Neuman, M. J. (2010). *Professionals in early childhood education and care systems: European profiles and perspectives*. Opladen and Farmington Hills: Barbara Budrich Publishers.

OECD (2012). *Research brief: qualifications, education and professional development matters.* Paris: OECD. Retrieved from: www.oecd.org/education/school/49322232.pdf.

Osgood, J. (2006). Deconstructing professionalism in early childhood education: resisting the regulatory gaze. *Contemporary Issues in Early Childhood,* 7(1), 5–14.

Peeters, J. & Vandenbroeck, M. (2011). Child care practitioners and the process of professionalisation. In L. Miller & C. Cable (Eds.), *Professionalisation and management in the early years.* London: Sage, pp. 62–74.

Penn, H. (2009). *Early childhood education and care: key lessons from research for policy makers.* Brussels: Nesse.

Penn, H. (forthcoming). The business of childcare in Europe. *European Eearly Childhood Education Research Journal,* DOI:10.1080/1350293X.2013.783300.

Pirard, F. (2005). Cultures de la qualité des services et cultures de l'accompagnement dans le secteur de l'éducation des jeunes enfants: essai de théorisation. Doctoral thesis. Liège. Université de Liège.

Pramling, N. & Pramling Samuelsson, I. (2011). *Education encounters: Nordic studies in early childhood didactics.* Dordrecht: Springer.

Šagud, M. (2008). Preparing Kindergarten Teachers for the Complex Field of Education. In I. Žogla (Ed.), *Teacher of the 21st century: quality education for quality teaching.* Riga: University of Latvia Press, pp. 169–175.

Slunjski, E. (2008). Professional development of educators aimed at research and change of their own educational practice. In I. Žogla (Ed.), *Teacher of the 21st century: quality education for quality teaching.* Riga: University of Latvia Press, pp. 707–713.

Stake, R. E. (2010). *Qualitative research: studying how things work.* New York: The Guilford Press.

Sylva, K., Melhuish, E., Sammons, P., Siraj-Blatchford, I. & Taggart, B. (2004). *The effective provision of preschool education (EPPE) project: final report.* Nothingham: DfES Publications and the Institute of Education.

Thomas, J. C. (2012). *Citizen, customer, partner: engaging the public in public management.* Armonk, NY: M.E. Sharpe.

Urban, M. (2007). Strategies for change: reflections from a systemic, comparative research project. In N. Hayes & S. Bradley (Eds.), *A decade of reflection early childhood care and education in Ireland: 1996–2006.* Dublin: Centre for Social and Educational Research.

Urban, M. (2012). Researching early childhood policy and practice: a critical ecology. *European Journal of Education,* 47, 494–507.

Urban, M., Vandenbroeck, M., Lazzari, A., Peeters, J. & Van Laere, K. (2011). *Competence requirements for early childhood education and care.* London and Ghent: UEL and UGent.

Urban, M., Vandenbroeck, M., Van Laere, K., Lazzari, A. & Peeters, J. (2012). Towards competent systems in ealry childhood education and care: implications for policy and practice. *European Journal of Education,* 47(4), 508–526.

Van Keulen, A. & Del Barrio, A. (2010). *Permanent leren: van zelfreflectie naar teamrefelectie.* Amsterdam: SWP.

Van Laere, K., Peeters, J. & Vandenbroeck, M. (2012). The education and care divide: the role of the early childhood workforce in 15 European countries. *European Journal of Education,* 47(4), 527–541.

Winnicot, D. W. (1987). *The child, the family and the outside world.* Cambridge: Perseus.

Wittorski, R. (2005). Des définitions s'imposent. In M. Sorel & R. Wittorski (Eds.), *La professionnalisation en actes et en questions.* Paris: L'Harmattan, pp. 183–210.

Žogla I. (Ed.) (2008) *Teacher of the 21st century: quality education for quality teaching.* Riga: University of Latvia Press.

1

THE DANISH PEDAGOGUE EDUCATION

Jytte Juul Jensen

Introduction

The Danish education of pedagogues has kept the idea of a special pedagogical identity for early childhood staff and, as a consequence, is quite distinct from the training for school teachers. This distinct training leads to qualification as a 'pedagogue', which are the core practitioners in early childhood centres, accounting for almost 60% of the staff. This chapter begins with a discussion of the difficulties concerning what English-language concepts and terms to use in discussing the education of pedagogues. The history of this education is then described, going from specialist to generalist before shifting back somewhat in 2014, and its close link to the early childhood welfare system, which has continuously expanded until today where there is universal coverage for all children from six months up to school age. The entry requirements for this educational course and the profile of pedagogue students in terms of age, sex and ethnicity are discussed, as well as the regulatory national framework for the education. Some key features of the education have been selected, in particular the aesthetic forms of expression, the activity and cultural subjects and the importance of placements.

A good professional, I will show, combines the academic and personal. While in a globalized world, acquiring intercultural competence is very important, and examples of how the education of pedagogues works with this issue are given.

Qualifying as a pedagogue

Denmark has had an education for the profession of pedagogue (*pædagog*) since 1992. In 2001, it became a professional bachelor degree and was last reformed in 2014. It is a three and a half year programme at higher education level.

I use the term 'pedagogue' instead of 'social educator', which is the official Danish translation. The ministerial decree uses the English name Bachelor's Degree Progamme in Social Education and the education validates the title Bachelor in Social Education (*Bekendtgørelse*, 2014) in Danish: *Professionsbachelor som pædagog*. I do not agree with the Danish translation, which is based on the assumption that the English vocabulary in educational issues does not use the Greek-based words 'pedagogues' or 'pedagogical work', while 'pedagogy' in English has a quite different meaning to its Danish use. During recent years those words have been seen more and more in English language academic books on education/training and on educational work with children, young people and adults.

The rejection of the words 'pedagogue' and 'pedagogical' may reflect an Anglo-American paradigm in early childhood practice and theory that is more school and curriculum oriented. The Anglo-American tradition has different historical roots than some continental European countries. The words 'pedagogue' and 'pedagogical', and their associated paradigms, are, however, well understood in many continental European countries, for example in Scandinavia and in countries whose national languages are rooted in Greek and Latin; these countries also share a Danish understanding of the term 'pedagogy'. This issue of language and language translation illustrates how difficult it is to make comparative work across countries and intercultural work, and how difficult it is to use English as one's working language.

From specialist to generalist to a mixture: history of the education of pedagogues

From an international perspective, continuity and tradition are key words to characterize the 130-year history of the education of pedagogues, although there have been many reforms during this time. There has been a continuous effort to raise the competence level of staff in early childhood centres and today 60% of the staff are pedagogues with a bachelor degree – a very high level compared to many countries in Europe (Oberhümer et al., 2010). Furthermore there has been a tradition of having a specific training separate from school teachers, with a generic pedagogue professional core that is applicable not only for working in early childhood centres but in many other welfare institutions.

The current Danish education of pedagogues, with its mixture of generalist and specialist, has its historical roots in three separate, specialized pedagogue educations: kindergarten pedagogue, leisure-time pedagogue and social pedagogue.

Education of kindergarten pedagogues

The first 'pedagogue' education dates back to 1885, where a course for staff in Fröbelkindergartens started. Later it became a one-year education for kindergarten teachers and in 1918 increased to two years. The education qualified pedagogues to work in kindergartens, with three to six-year old children.

Education of leisure-time pedagogues

Initially, this education was integrated into the kindergarten pedagogue education. But the first specific courses for this area of work started in 1945, and later a specific leisure-time pedagogue education were established. The educational course qualifies pedagogues to work in leisure centres, clubs and other types of service for school children and young people up to around 20 years of age.

Education of social pedagogues

The third specialist pedagogue education was that for social pedagogues, originally split up into several aspects targeting specific occupational areas. Not until 1958 did an education come about specifically for child welfare pedagogue, which took one year and increased later to two and then three years. In 1974 all the different educational courses merged into 'child welfare- and care pedagogue', which two years later became 'social pedagogue'. This qualified pedagogues for work in residential institutions for children and young people, in day and residential services for people with disabilities and for people with social problems; it was also a qualification for work in centres for children under three years of age. The age range for which the social pedagogues were trained was from birth to 99.

In 1970 the education of kindergarten and leisure-time pedagogues, and some years later child welfare- and care pedagogues, were extended to three years, and in 1974 upgraded from short to medium cycle further higher education. This reflected the development of welfare institutions and a general increase in educational levels in Denmark.

In 1992 the three pedagogue educations merged into a single education. The main reason for this was that employers did not pay attention to the specific type of specialized qualification held by job applicants, so the occupational field had in practice already merged. Another reason was the emergence of new types of work areas for pedagogues. In addition, a generalist education gave pedagogues the possibility of moving between different pedagogical work fields during their careers. One of the reasons why the pedagogue profession has attracted a relatively high number of men has to do with this generalist approach.

In 2001 the education of pedagogues was upgraded to bachelor level. A reform was made in 2007 re-introducing a mild degree of specialization. A reform in 2014 has taken this process further, turning towards a more specialized pedagogue education. The education today consists of two parts: a common part on basic professional competences (70 ECTS) and a specialization part (140 ECTS), so it combines a generalist first year with subsequent specialization into either early childhood pedagogy; school and leisure pedagogy; or social and special pedagogy.

The Danish early childhood pedagogical system

The list below gives an overview of the early childhood pedagogical system in Denmark. Denmark provides early childhood services for all children and now offers nearly universal coverage. Each child has the right to a place, if their parents wish it. Access to universal early childhood services has been realized through extensive public commitments to funding, legislation and running the services. This has to be understood within the Scandinavian welfare system, with rapid expansion of services from the mid-1960s, connected with the increase in female employment. Denmark has one of the highest employment rates for mothers in the EU – both fathers and mothers work and most mothers work almost full time, which is 37 hours per week. A high level of tax-based public funding exists. The legal framework on early childhood services is under the auspices of the Ministry for Children, Gender Equality, Integration and Social Affairs. The responsibilities to provide and fund early childhood services are delegated to the 98 local authorities.

The early childhood pedagogical system in Denmark:

- Statutory school starting age: six years.
- Universal entitlement to a fee-paying full-time place in an early childhood facility from the age of six months.
- Unitary system of ministerial responsibility from birth to five years under the auspices of the Ministry for Children, Gender Equality, Integration and Social Affairs (returned to Social Affairs in 2013 following two years under Education).
- Both age-integrated (from birth to five years) and age-separated (from birth to two years, three to five years) centres.
- Municipal family daycare is part of the system. 48% of enrolled children under three years attend a family day carer.
- Majority of service providers public/municipal (81%); 16% private non-profit and 3% private for-profit (2013).
- Percentage of children under three in early childhood formal settings: 68% (2013).
- Percentage of children between three years and statutory school age: 97% (2013).

(Danmarks Statistik, 2014)

Staff in early childhood centres:

- Job title of core practitioner in Danish: *pædagog*.
- Required qualification: bachelor degree.
- Professional education with a basic year followed by a choice of three specialization areas, one in early years provision. The education takes place at University Colleges.
- Duration of education (full-time equivalent): three and a half years.
- Supported by auxiliary staff (*pædagogmedhjælpere*, literally 'pedagogical co-helpers') without a required qualification.
- Proportion of staff with a higher education qualification: 58% (2013).

(Danmarks Statistik, 2014)

As seen in the above list the staffing of early childhood services consists of two occupational groups working in centre-based institutions: pedagogues and 'pedagogical co-helpers' (*pædagogmedhjælpere*) literally translated. There is no clear distinction concerning the tasks or functions between the two groups. Pedagogues have overall responsibility, including the right to delegate pedagogical learning processes to the co-helpers.

Almost all heads/leaders of the centres are qualified pedagogues. It is considered a benefit that those leading the work are qualified in the profession. Arguably, only in this way can the head/leader understand the occupational field.

Since the 1970s, the decision-making structure in Danish early childhood centres has been flat and non-hierarchal. Recently, there has been some reversal in this characteristic of Danish centres, as heads have been upgraded, partly because they are the group of pedagogues that has had most post-graduate qualifications. The heads/leaders have also become more and more conscious of the difference between pedagogues and pedagogical co-helpers.

During their education pedagogues have gained knowledge, skills and competences to carry out pedagogical work in a variety of pedagogical institutions and settings. The overall aims for the pedagogues are decided in different welfare acts. Pedagogical work is community work, and pedagogues carry out work for society, which has laid down certain aims for this work. In the act on early childhood services (*Dagtilbudsloven*, 2015) several aims are specified for all institutions in Denmark. In addition, local authorities must by law have a coherent children policy, in which further aims and tasks are defined for local pedagogical services. Often local authorities also have a specific early childhood policy and certain specific areas to which pedagogues must pay special attention. Last but not least, the individual institutions have their own written learning plans. Pedagogues must take account of all these considerations when acting in their practice.

Entry requirements

Each year the Ministry of Education decides the number of pedagogue students to be recruited. The entry requirements are based on a quota system. Quota 1 takes in students with the highest grade in upper secondary examination. Minimum age of entry is 18 years, with 12 years of schooling and an upper secondary leaving certificate. Quota 2 makes possible a variety of entry routes based on assessment of competences and qualifications. These varied entry requirements and routes ensure a varied student intake.

One entry route is the merit-based bachelor programme aimed at experienced but untrained workers; this offers pedagogical co-helpers a chance to become qualified pedagogues. It is equivalent to 150 ECTS points, after achieving which students are awarded the title of pedagogue, having been credited for their previous practical experience with pedagogical work. Oberhümer, Schreyer and Neuman (2010) characterize this entry route as 'an inclusive approach, with flexible entry routes for mature students with prior learning and employment experience' (p. 108).

The pedagogue education is a popular choice and an attractive profession among young people in Denmark. Each year around 5,000 students are enrolled and many are rejected, so there is no recruitment problem in Denmark. In terms of numbers, it is the largest higher education sector in the country. There are no tuition fees for the course as is the case for most higher education in Denmark. During their studies the students receive from central government a student grant of 791 EUR a month, which may be supplemented by a loan of 409 EUR a month (2015 figures). Most students also work part time, many in pedagogical settings, in order to cover their living expenses and have a reasonable standard of living.

The age, sex and ethnicity profile of pedagogue students

Pedagogue students in Denmark differ widely in terms of age, sex and ethnicity. The average age of students, when they start the course, is relatively high. Fifteen years ago it was around 27 years of age, but this figure has fallen.

The education of pedagogues has been able to attract a relatively large number of male students, 25% of the total currently, the highest percentage ever. Male pedagogues do not work in large numbers in early childhood centres, preferring out-of-school facilities, clubs, residential care and services for adults with disabilities. The percentage of male workers in centres for children under three years is only 7%. In centres for three to six year old children and in age-integrated institutions for children from birth to six years old, it is a bit higher, at 11% and 13% respectively (*Danmarks Statistik*, 2010).

Those percentages, however, also include pedagogue co-helpers, and many institutions prefer to employ young male workers in this role. According to BUPL[1], in 2014 only 37 male pedagogues were working in centres for under threes, which is just 2.7% of the total number of pedagogues, with 542 in centres for children over three and 1,122 in centres for children from birth to six years of age, almost 7% of all pedagogues for both types (Larsen, 2015).

The education of pedagogues has also been able to attract ethnic minority students, both male and female, who account for about 5% of all students. This is partly because of a specific pre-course for students from a non-Danish ethnic background.

Regulatory framework in providing the pedagogue education

Historically education of pedagogues took place at a higher education college specializing in this. This was also the case for other professional higher education programmes, for example for teachers, social workers and nurses. In 2000 there were 32 pedagogue colleges in Denmark. Today the former smaller specialized colleges are grouped into seven larger units called University Colleges (*profession-shøjskoler*), offering a variety of bachelor programmes for professional education, including the pedagogue education. The education programmes are recognized and financed by the Ministry of Education and Research. The Ministry provides a subsidy to cover direct teaching costs, a so-called 'taximeter subsidy' per student laid down in the yearly Finance Act.

The 2014 ministerial decree (*Bekendtgørelse*, 2014) on the study programme for the award of Bachelor in Social Education regulates the pedagogue education in Denmark and is supplemented by each University College's specific course syllabus. Individual University Colleges, therefore, have substantial freedom to develop local variations in their study programmes.

§1 of the ministerial decree states: 'The purpose of the education is that the student acquires relevant professional competences, knowledge and skills, to be able to manage, develop and convey development, learning and care assignments in a social perspective, both independently and in collaboration with others'.

The pedagogue training programme takes, as before, three and a half years of full-time study and amounts to 210 ECTS credits. The degree is on a par with other professional bachelor programmes as for example teachers, social workers and nurses.

The education consists of two parts: a common part on basic professional competences (70 ECTS points) and a specialization part (140 ECTS points). In the common part there is a placement period of 10 ECTS points.

The student must in the specialization part choose between:

1. Early childhood pedagogy, aimed at pedagogical work with children aged from birth to five years.
2. School and leisure pedagogy, aimed at pedagogical work with school children and young people aged between six and eighteen years.
3. Social and special pedagogy, aimed at pedagogical work with children and young people with special needs and people with physical or mental disabilities or social problems.

The specialization course also consists of an inter-professional course, a bachelor project and three placement periods.

Pedagogues specialized in early childhood pedagogy:

> have particular competences to create and develop pedagogical environments and activities, in which optimal conditions are created on the basis of a professional, pedagogical foundation for a stimulating and safe life for children.

Competence areas are:

1. Childhood, culture and learning.
2. Profession and organization
3. Professional relations and communication – 2nd placement period.
4. Cooperation and development – 3rd placement period.

(Bekendtgørelse, 2014. Appendix 2)

The competence area on childhood, culture and learning is the specific academic knowledge base for the early childhood staff, and the decree states that:

> This area aims at the inclusion of culture, nature and aesthetic forms of expression in pedagogical activities that support children's development, intellectual growth and learning.
>
> Competence goals: The student is able to utilize nature, as well as cultural media and forms of expression to create developmental and learning processes for 0–5 year old children, and furthermore to incorporate the perspective of children into play and pedagogical activities.
>
> *(Bekendtgørelse, 2014)*

The following section will go into more details about the place in pedagogue education of aesthetic forms of expression.

Aesthetic forms of expression

Aesthetic forms of expression in pedagogical activities have always played a major role in the Danish education of pedagogues. The students must have aesthetic competences in carrying out activities and must participate in them themselves (with their bodies). They must have practical skills, which they learn not only on placements but also at the University College.

When the pedagogue student is on a placement, it is not only a question of observing, but also a question of her personal formation (*dannelse* in Danish, *Bildung* in German), so the student develops skills and competences based in her own body. In this way a pedagogue can influence and work with children, young people and adults. Behind this lies a democratic understanding of responsibility. To work closely with children and young people and to make sure that everybody can participate as a citizen, the pedagogue must find the resources everybody has, which cannot be done theoretically.

Children and pedagogues must be together about something. To participate in communities about something or with something, which means creating culture, is something the Danish education system values highly. Here the aesthetic learning processes are important. It is underlined that children can express themselves; and not only express themselves according to certain norms but they must be able to express themselves, experiment and play in their own ways. This means that pedagogues, as their starting point, take those processes and actions children that are in. In the Danish view, children are agentic and are already in action. They are no empty vessels.

The pedagogue must be able to notice and get permission to participate in what children are already doing and must also have competences to qualify what children are doing. Here lies an ambivalence: on the one hand to take as a starting point what children already can and will do, but on the other hand to socialize them into and take the community into consideration.

During their studies at the University College, the pedagogue students must try out how to achieve aesthetic skills. This is a different type of learning process than the cognitive one. The students must achieve skills in, for example, playing an instrument, telling a story, balancing a ball, playing in a sandbox, lighting a bonfire, climbing a tree and so on. They must practice during their studies – for practice makes perfect! If you are good at something you also bring something into the community as yourself. Pedagogues must have those skills and competences because, if you do, the children like to be together with you.

In Danish pedagogy literature such activities are referred to as the common third, a concept introduced by Michael Husen (1985), a Danish philosopher. The concept indicates that the activity is neither only the adults' nor the children's but something beyond, where both adults and children are absorbed and have shared ownership. Others talk about the good otherness, a concept elaborated by Thomas Ziehe (2004), a German philosopher, who has had much influence on Danish youth pedagogy.

During the three and a half years years of the pedagogue study programme the students get personal formation linked to the processes where they become aware of, open up for, and get her/his own interests qualified and in the end achieve the aesthetic skills. This takes place during the different activities and cultural subjects. Some students experience this as contrary to their idea of higher education, as they believe that to learn and study is to sit on a chair and read.

The priority given to this work is also seen in the physical layout of the University Colleges. Here you find handicrafts areas, gymnasiums, drama and music rooms, photo and IT rooms, wood and metal rooms, and outdoor facilities. All rooms are well equipped with relevant materials – so here the students must try things out. They must learn how they themselves can participate in the activities and the daily life at the early childhood centres.

Placement[2]

The education of pedagogues has always made placements in future work settings a relatively large part of the study programme. There is a strong interplay between learning in an educational institution and learning in a pedagogical workplace, which give two different learning spaces that are of equal significance for the students. It is important to underline that college education is not only theory and workplace education is not only practice (Bayer, 2000). For example practical skills, as described above, are an important part of college time.

The ministerial decree sets out the formal framework for placements. There are four placement periods equivalent in total to 75 ECTS points. The first placement takes place as part of the general course; the next two, each lasting half a year, are specialization placements; and the fourth placement is part of the bachelor project. The students are supervised by a pedagogue at the early years' centre as well as a teacher from the University College.

Different understandings about placement have dominated at different periods during the 130 year history of pedagogue education. Højbjerg (2007, pp. 8–13) identifies four key understandings. The first two are referred to as paradigms and the last two as discourses, as they are variations of the first two.

- Placement as training of practical skills – a work paradigm
- Placement as applying theory in practice – a scholastic paradigm
- Placement as a space for learning – a learning discourse
- Placement as a space for creating knowledge – an academic discourse.

Today the two last discourses exist side by side. The learning discourse is about how to master and understand the practice of the pedagogue profession; and the academic discourse is about how to gain and produce knowledge. The 2014 study programme can be seen as integrating the two discourses even more, which brings challenges to both the University Colleges and the early childhood centres.

Personal and academic competences: a good professional

In Denmark it is common to talk about the three Ps: professional, personal and private. The reason is to underline the demarcation between personal and private. A good pedagogue must be personal and must make an appreciative relation to children but in doing so not become private. Figure 1.1 expands the concepts to include dogmatism. Personal competences and specific academic knowledge constitute the good professional pedagogue, but a demarcation is made between the private and the dogmatic.

During her three and a half years' education, the pedagogue becomes competent in the specific academic knowledge base, values and ethos of the pedagogue profession. But a pedagogue must also work with her personal competences. These include her own life experiences, her engagement and corporeality, her feelings and own values and morals.

The Danish education of pedagogues attaches importance to the student's personal formation during the three and a half year year course. Students must have both an academic and a personal education formation, which is very much linked to the body and corporeality. To be trustworthy as a pedagogue one must dare to invest one's own personality in the work, one way or the other, to make appreciative relationships. Pedagogues can use personal experiences if they are able to generalize them and make them academic. How to use personal experiences is very much about a sense of the individual situation.

| Private | Personal | Academic knowledge | Dogmatism |

The professional pedagogue

FIGURE 1.1 The private, personal, academic knowledge and dogmatism

Regarding the personal, a demarcation is drawn between what is private. The norm and ideal of the pedagogues' culture is to be personal (to relate) and academic, but to avoid the private. This demarcation between what is private is substantial. The private is here understood not so much as about the pedagogue's private life and own life experiences, than as about the pedagogue's own needs and feelings, which must not rule relations with the child or children. Also eventual non-worked with conflicts or non-conscious needs among the pedagogue are part of the private. The demarcation line between personal and private is not only to protect the pedagogue but also the child, and is thereby an ethical question (Mørch, 2007).

Another important distinction is between the specific knowledge of the profession and a dogmatic, one-sided knowledge. Danish pedagogy does not build on one single theoretical position, nor is pedagogy practiced by the rule-book and following prescriptive guidelines. Rather, pedagogical practice is built on judgment in the individual situation, drawing on many sources of knowledge, and does not base its knowledge on a one-sided pedagogical school of thought.

Intercultural competence and the international

In the Danish Government's publication *Fremgang, fornyelse og tryghed*, which presents the government's globalization strategy, the term 'intercultural compe-tence' is used. Here it is formulated as a political request that different educations must all strengthen knowledge and competences that shall 'be a good basis for dialogue and interaction with other cultures' (Cirius 2007; taken from Day & Steensen, 2010). Day and Steensen, editors of a recent book on intercultural competences, point out specific conditions that dominate in the educational sec-tor, which are, 'that there is a need that not only the professionals (teachers/ pedagogues) themselves possess intercultural competences but they should also be able to organize processes, by means of which their pupils/students/children/ young people develop those competences' (2010, p. 7).

Concurrently with globalization, the pedagogue profession is faced with new challenges and tasks that demand intercultural competences. Today Danish society is a multicultural society, including a number of groups whose cultural backgrounds are other than Danish. Around 10–15% of children in early childhood centres come from a minority ethnic background. Moreover, pedagogues, like other peo-ple, are woven into different international relations, which may be expressed in various ways: as professionals they visit early childhood centres abroad, participate in international conferences or get inspired by academic literature and practice from abroad. Some pedagogues also get a job abroad.

Pedagogical work is community work where the overall aims and frame-works are laid down at central and local level. And the work is influenced by the current policy agendas. This is also the case for intercultural work. Citizens whose background is not Danish are often subjected to negative stories in the media, and there are huge political differences in attitudes towards these citizens. This means that pedagogues are challenged in how they will work with the intercultural. Therefore, according to Day and Steensen, it is important to know 'which political discourses influence the practice of the profession', and also to know 'where the discourses are inconsistent with the profession's own norms and values' (Ibid., p. 8).

The authors end their introduction by saying that the intercultural competences of professionals as pedagogues, teachers, social workers etc. have 'two dimensions: both an ability to know how to function adequately in complex cultural contexts – and an ability to know how to state the reasons for one's actions' (Ibid. p. 15).

In the education as a pedagogue, intercultural competences have over the years played a major role. Some University Colleges have a building-bridge course, which is an access or pre-course for people with minority ethnic backgrounds. Most of the students on these courses continue on to enter pedagogue education. This means that both fellow students as well as college teachers – professionally and personally – must take into consideration how to deal with the issue of meeting people from another cultural background.

One way of building up the students' intercultural competences is to study abroad. Most popular is the possibility of taking one of the half year placements in another country, which is a right stipulated in the ministerial decree. In the University College where I worked around 20–25% of the students make use of this opportunity, with placement institutions based all over the world and covering all types of pedagogical work. To study at a University abroad is also a possibility.

Many University Colleges have students attending from abroad who often follow a specially designed module for three to six months, and some colleges run courses abroad. To have students from abroad is another way of creating a more intercultural environment at a college, making possible meetings between teachers, Danish students and students from abroad.

Such examples provide rich opportunities for students to have intercultural meetings. But they are not the only fora for achieving intercultural competences. The students also study ethnic minority issues during teaching sessions at college, as well as in their project work and placements.

Different research projects show that ethnic classifications and categorizations are constructed all the time by pedagogues and in their practice, often behind 'their back' (Larsen, 2010). Ethnicity is often a category used to explain the behaviour or actions among ethnic minority children instead of looking at each individual child and its concrete relationships and at the practice in the institution. In her anthropological study in a Danish institution, Palludan (2008) identifies two types of tone that pedagogues use in their communication with children: a tone of teaching and a tone of exchange. The pedagogues in general use the tone of teaching in their communication with ethnic minority children.

Also the classification and categorization of children according to their disadvantaged social background is common among pedagogues and this issue is also worked with during the pedagogue education. Gender is another classification, but is less prominent on the pedagogical agenda.

Concluding remarks

The Danish education of pedagogues has a 130 year history, and during all this time has kept the idea of a distinct form of pedagogical thinking for early childhood centres, which as a consequence has created an education separate from that for school teachers. The training has on the contrary been linked, merged and today mixes with that for out-of-school facilities, residential homes and day and residential centres for disabled people. Another continuous feature is that it has been considered important that the education of staff in early childhood centres is of the utmost importance for the quality of services and today almost 60% of staff are pedagogues with a bachelor degree – a high percentage compared to many countries in Europe and elsewhere.

The pedagogue education is the most popular choice in higher education among young people in Denmark and recruitment and retention is not an issue. It has succeeded in attracting many male and ethnic minority students. There are several reasons for this: the bachelor degree level education, inclusive entry routes to education, steady jobs in welfare institutions and job mobility between different types of institutions.

Early childhood centres form a huge area in the welfare state and the pedagogue education has a close link to them, as well as other welfare institutions. A continuous development of early childhood centres over many years to their universal coverage today is another important factor in the development of the education of pedagogues, as these centres have needed trained pedagogues. A close link has existed between training and jobs.

The importance of public commitment, including funding for both the education of pedagogues and the early childhood centres, is of the uttermost importance in maintaining continuity and quality.

The present chapter has underlined the importance of the aesthetic forms of expression to the pedagogical identity of early childhood education. Appropriate training facilities, such as rooms for creative workshops, drama, music, movement, IT and much more are available at University Colleges so the students can practice their aesthetic competences. Placements have always been a strong basis of the education of pedagogues, showing the close relation between the early childhood workplace and the training institutes.

A good professional, combining both the academic and the personal, has been analysed. In a globalized world it is very important that the students acquire intercultural competence as they will meet people from many cultural backgrounds. Some examples of how University Colleges are working with this issue are given. Many students, for example, grasp the opportunity to take one of their half-year placements abroad to experience first-hand how to relate to another culture.

Notes

1 BUPL is the trade union for the trained staff - the pedagogues - in nurseries, kindergartens, age-integrated centres, out-of-school facilities and leisure time centres, as well as leisure time and youth clubs.
2 For further reading see Jensen, 2015.

References

Bayer, M. (2000). Mødet med praksis: i praktikken. *Vera*, 12, 11–27.

Bekendtgørelse om uddannelsen til professionsbachelor som pædagog: Bek. nr. 211 af 06/03/2014. Copenhagen: Uddannelses- og Forskningsministeriet (Ministerial Decree on Study Programme for Bachelor in Social Education).

Dagtilbudsloven (2015). Lov nr. 167 af 20/02/2015. Copenhagen: Ministeriet for Børn, Ligestilling, Integration og Sociale forhold.

Danmarks Statistik (2010). Børnepasning mv. efteråret 2009. *Statistiske Efterretninger* 2010, p. 2. Copenhagen: Danmarks Statistik.

Danmarks Statistik (2014). Børnepasning mv. efteråret 2013. *Statistiske Efterretninger* 2014, p. 2. Copenhagen: Danmarks Statistik.

Day, B. & Steensen, J. (2010). Interkulturel kompetence som dimension i professionsud-vikling. In B. Day & J. Steensen (Eds.), *Kultur og etnicitet på arbejde*, pp. 7–16. Århus: VIA Systime.

Højbjerg, B. (2007). Praktik og etnografisk feltarbejde. In P. Mikkelsen & S. Holm-Larsen (Eds.), *Praktik i pædagoguddannelsen*, pp. 7–27. Frederikshavn: Dafolo.

Husen, M. (1985). *Socialpædagogik og arbejdsprocesser.* Copenhagen: Socialpædagogernes Faglige organisation.

Jensen, J. J. (2015). Placement supervision of pedagogue students in Denmark: the role of university colleges and early childhood centres. *Early Years*, 35(2), 154–167, http://dx.doi.org/10.1080/09575146.2015.1024616.

Larsen, V. (2010). Kategoriseringer i en multikulturel praksis. In B. Day & J. Steensen (Eds.), *Kultur og etnicitet på arbejde*, pp. 101–123; Århus: VIA Systime.

Larsen, T. V. (2015). Henrik blev vild med vuggestuen. *Børn & Unge*, 6, 3

Mørch, S. I. (2007). *Individ, institution og samfund: pædagogiske perspektiver.* Viborg: Academica.

Oberhümer, P. Schreyer, I. & Neuman, M. J. (2010). *Professionals in early childhood education and care systems: European profiles and perspectives.* Opladen: Barbara Budrich.

Palludan, C. (2008). *Børnehaven gør en forskel.* Copenhagen: Danmarks Pædagogiske Universitets Forlag.

Ziehe, T. (2004). *Øer af intensitet i et hav af rutine.* Copenhagen: Politisk revy.

2

A TRAINING FOR EARLY CHILDHOOD EDUCATORS COMBINED WITH FULL-TIME EMPLOYMENT IN LYON

Marie Paule Thollon Behar and Myriam Mony

Introduction

Early childhood education and care (ECEC) in France is characterised by a great variety of different professionals, each with a different training (Mony, 2002). Despite the heterogeneity of the workforce, and despite the prevailing discourses on lifelong learning, there are very limited possibilities for horizontal or vertical job mobility. The *Ecole de Santé Sociale du Sud-Est* in Lyon (France) offers a special qualifying training, which enables professionals with low qualifications to enter a graduating course and obtain the diploma of *éducateur jeunes enfants* (early childhood educator, further EJE), a three-year long, post secondary school diploma, while remaining in their employment during the entire training. We will further refer to these trainees as "salaried students".

The EJE have a particular role in the child care services. Often, they are in charge of the pedagogical dimension of the team. They can also be the manager of the team (Ministère de l'emploi et de la solidarité, 2000). As a consequence, the EJE training for professionals with low qualifications enables them to access a more valorised profession and higher salaries. It is to be noted that it follows the model of a *diplôme d'état* (State diploma), meaning that the training centres prepare students for a state examination but do not assess the students (as this is the monopoly of the state). Nevertheless, all students so far have successfully passed the diploma tests (Mony, 2013).

All professional training in early childhood care, education and social work, from the health and social ministry in France are based on work-linked training (except the assistants: "*CAP petite enfance*" and childminders who have a limited training of 120 hours). In the special case of the training discussed here, where students remain paid and in full-time employment, there are particular opportunities and challenges in relating theory and practice. As the CoRe research concludes: the relationship between theory and practice is an essential tool to support the reflexive competencies of the team (Urban et al., 2011). Yet, in order to have a successful relation between theory and practice, certain conditions need to be met, taking into account the interactions between the different actors in the field: trainers, employers, managers, students and colleagues. Special attention is also devoted to what is called the *analyse des pratiques* (analyses of daily practices) as a method to construct this relation.

Three decades of experience with this training and the case study made for the CoRe research show that the four dimensions of the competent system, described in the final report are involved: individual level, institution and team level, inter-institution level and political level. We first present the context of the training, its origins, and its governance, referring to the levels of inter-institutional collaboration and governance, as mentioned in the conclusions of the CoRe research.

Then we present the results of the case study, based on interviews of students, professionals and managers. This part refers to the level of individual competences and to the institutional level of team competences. The case study also provides insights into the conditions for success. Finally, we deepen a central aspect of the pedagogy to co-construct competences in the relation between theory and practice: the analysis of practices.

The context: inter-institution and policy competences

In 1988 the *Association des Collectifs Enfants Parents Professionnels* (ACEPP), a French national network of about 1,000 parent-led day care centres (*crèches parentales*) initiated a qualification process for its young employees without diploma: the EJE. Among its unique features was a systemic conception of alternated training for employees and a pedagogy of balanced alternation between the professional fields and the training centres. The training aimed at the development of professional competences in a context of shortage, and to promote professionalisation, while the parent-led crèches mushroomed and grew from 100 day care centres in 1981 to 1,100 in 1991, meaning that over 300 young graduate EJEs were trained in five years.

The EJE is a bachelor-level diploma in social and educational work that prepares those who qualify with it to work with children outside of the school context. From the start, the national network of ACEPP negotiated with policy makers on inclusive measures to enable youngster who had previously dropped out to access higher education through the recognition of acquired competences. As a result, funding was made available for training and for inter-institutional coordination between all partners of this inclusive training project. This included eight training centres; the regional coordination centres of ACEPP; and specifically for Lyon, the *Collège Cooperatif Rhône-Alpes,* a training centre specialised in including workers with limited initial education and working in close cooperation with the *Ecole de Santé Sociale du Sud-Est* (ESSSE) to develop projects that alternate between work and training.

Since this project, ESSSE as well as other centres in France in this field have continued to develop such training devices with local partners. Because of its unique possibilities in offering a specialised bachelor course in early childhood education, accessible for early years workers, even when these have very limited formal education, the ESSSE was selected as a case study in the CoRe research. ESSSE yearly serves 85 regular students and an additional 30 "salaried students": early years workers who alternate their work with the qualifying EJE training.

The organisation of the training

The training enables early childhood staff to go for a qualification without leaving their jobs. The employer and/or the state provide the funding, although this may be difficult to obtain and the professional may have to wait several years before receiving it. The students can enter the training through a competitive intake examination, which is the same for all future students. The salaried students stay together in a separate group and do not mix with the "regular" students. They benefit from a specific pedagogy, as they alternate three weeks per month at work and a week in the training centre. During the training, a *tutor*, who is an educator in the employer's team (and thus a colleague at the workplace), accompanies the student. A *reference trainer* supports the student in the training centre. At the end of the training, all students, whether regular or salaried, will take the same state exam at the same time. Even though the salaried students started the training with a lower level, their results are evaluated in the same way and their results are comparable with those of the regular students.

The salaried students have the same curriculum as the regular students but trainers accompany them in separate groups; this enables the trainers to adapt the pedagogy to their specific situation (Pueyo, 2004). More specifically, being in a separate group enables the teachers to devise the learning experience in relation with practice through group support of the process of training, a group of analyses of practices and workshops on pedagogical practices. There are two additional groups for the salaried students: one to support writing capacities and one on computer use. Considering that some of the salaried students left school at an early age, these additional groups support them to improve their academic levels. The trainers follow up the students in very individualised ways and they visit the students at their workplaces four times during the three years of training.

An in-depth case study

After these more structural and governance levels, we will now turn to the individual and institutional levels: the development of a pedagogical link between theory and practice, the construction of a professional identity and the relations among students as well as between students and their teams. What follows is based on an in-depth case study comprising individual and small-group interviews with students, day care managers and trainers. The aim was to determine, from the point of view of each interviewed person, how the training contributes to competence building, its interest, its limits and the conditions of success. The research was conducted at the Lyon-based school for higher education ESSSE.

The interviewees included six students during the second year of training; six managers of day care centres; two trainers for early childhood educators; and one trainer who served as a referent person for the students. A thematic analysis of the interviews revealed two dimensions: the dimension of the student, his or her experience and how he or she is building competences; and the dimension of the team and the effects produced, over the three years, by the presence of a colleague who is following a training qualification.

Developing competences from experience

The students unanimously said that the training makes it possible to link theory and practice. They all have a working experience in early childhood education and care and therefore the theoretical contents make sense to them:

> When we take a course, we immediately make links; we are immediately put in a reflection process. (…) Our experience enables us to concretely understand such points considered in the theoretical session.
>
> *(Student)*

The theoretical approach makes sense when it is based on experience. The knowledge process becomes easier because it is based on a strong practice. As one student expressed it:

> Expressing my practice in words has helped me turn it into skills.

The transformation of experience from practice into competencies is key in adult education (Barbier & Galatanu, 2004; Barbier, 2011). But it also includes a phase of destabilisation: all training has a phase of disturbance, when previous knowledge and previous experiences are questioned and deconstructed in order to build new competences and insights. This is even truer for the salaried students, who have more experience, yet are expected to question this experience. It is often questioned whether the level of competences acquired by salaried students matches the level of the regular students. Can it create some "low cost" training? For the interviewed students, there is a difference in the professional process:

> The work experience gives more maturity, which enables us to build our professionalism, through different pathways, compared to the classical training.
>
> *(Student)*

The trainers confirm that the level that the salaried students acquire is to be compared with that of the regular students, despite the fact that their starting level is often lower. They ascertain that the training succeeds in providing professional development for persons who did not have the initial resources (or required levels of education) to enrol in regular early childhood education training.

> For the test on pedagogy, which is really the core of the job, they are excellent; they can perfectly show the link between theory and practice, because we had worked on it during all the training.
>
> *(Trainer)*

After qualifying, the students can be educators, but can also become managers. In that position, they know well the roles and missions of each member of the team, because they were one of them before taking up a management position.

> I think that this training is bringing different competences, because we keep our initial competences that are not the same. We do not have the same point of view; it is expanding competences that are different from the classical training.
>
> For those who have the double qualification assistant-educator, and are in the position of management, I have seen persons very efficiently demonstrating the competence to initiate collaboration, and to support complementarity. Especially in our sector, that is very complex. They are 'hybrid' professionals that are in the recognition of the two functions.
>
> *(Trainer)*

Yet, in order to be able to build these complex competences of the hybrid professional, students need to profoundly question their professional identity.

Changes in professional identity

The challenge is that students need to acquire a diploma for their job mobility, while being salaried in their initial work. This means that their professional identity has to change over the three and half years, while in their practice, for their team and for both the colleagues and the employer, they keep the same professional position. It is a delicate balance for the person who undergoes these changes and it is always a source of internal, and inter-relational conflicts, as we will see later. The training group is one way to build this hybrid professional identity. The combination of three weeks of work and one week in training requires a constant gymnastic between the positions of student and professional team member. The professional identity changes during the training sessions and during the exchanges. But when the student turns back to work, she or he is reintegrating with the team in the same position as before.

> In my team, I am salaried like an *auxilière* (literally auxiliary, it is the term used in France to designate early years staff with a vocational education level), I have to do my job as an auxiliary assistant (…). You change during the training, but when you go back, you are still an animator.
>
> *(Salaried student)*

> The manager said to me: there is yet an educator in this team, you have to keep your position of assistant.
>
> *(Salaried student)*

Despite these potential difficulties, a salaried student testified as to the success of the combination work/training:

> I appreciated the combination. In the beginning, I needed time to adapt myself, to find my references when I went back to work. But, when I finally found the balance between work and training, I found a great interest in the combination. I liked to leave work for the week at the training centre. On the other hand, I was happy to come back to work at the end of the week.
>
> *(Student)*

The trainers assert that changing from the position of educator to the position of manager can entail jealousy and rivalry in the team. It is a switch that the salaried student could experience as a conflict of loyalty with his or her colleagues. In addition, the student needs to find the right place between being employed and being in training, since the workplace is used as a training place too (i.e. as an internship site). This enables learning about different roles, missions, and competences as an ECEC educator. However, the student must be able to comprehend the difference in status between an employee and a student in order to know how to behave consequently and – as a result – needs to discover other aspects of his or her future job. That is not always easy:

> It was difficult for me to consider myself as a trainee on my work place. The amount of daily work doesn't leave much time to observe, experiment and to think and elaborate projects.
>
> *(Student)*

> One must be ready to accept and change because the training changes people.
>
> *(Student)*

The latter statement suggests that the training does not only involve a change in professional identity, but also in personal identity. First, because during the training:

> We have to wear many hats: employee, trainee, student, even mother for some of us. You need to adapt yourself.
>
> *(Student)*

The change of professional identity impacts the image of the person. The changes in social identity (going from a very low educational level to the bachelor diploma of an educator) may impact the personal life and may lead to marital tensions and even divorce.

Conditions for success from the student's point of view

A specific training system is put in place to successfully combine theory and practice in ways that lead to competence building. It is based on *analyse de la pratique*: the reflection upon practice, a reflection in reference groups, supported by the trainers and by the accompanying tutor. It truly is a co-construction of knowledge. The reference groups meet each time they are back at the training centre. These moments are places for pooling and sharing experiences. They offer a broader vision of professional activities, considering the variety of workplaces where the students are employed. The group is also a support during a difficult training:

> It's clear that, if we don't get along, it can be difficult… There are ups and downs, but, individually, when things go wrong, these moments are very supportive.
>
> *(Student)*

During each training session, the students take part in the analysis of the practices group. A psychologist coaches the group. It is a time to work on affects linked to experiences lived in the training, to go deeper into the analysis of the situations, and to make sense of the practices, in relation with theory. It is also a time to work on the dimension of the relationships with colleagues, manager and trainers.

All such analyses are supervised by a referent trainer. This referent trainer is in charge of the guidance of the group but he or she also accompanies each student individually during the entire training. She or he visits the student on his or her workplace and may take a regulatory role between the team and the student when necessary. This support is also important during the periods in the training centre, to help the students coping with the training requirements both on the professional and the personal levels.

Team competences: the impact on the workplace

All interviewees (students and managers) unanimously say that the team benefits from the training of one of its members, in terms of competence improvements. First, the team is involved in the questioning and reflection that forms the basis of the training process. Moreover, the team also integrates the reflection of the salaried student, including new ideas. The new light that the student sheds on the practices may help the team to take a critical distance from the usual experiences.

Beyond the questioning, the contribution of knowledge and methodology is also appreciated by the team. Legitimised by the reference to the training centre, the student is considered as a resource person for theoretical contents and for methodology, particularly when observation is concerned:

> She has brought us other ways of practising, based on theory. She has handed out some documents in relation to the points chosen by the team and she could explain them.
>
> *(Manager)*

The result is an improvement of the quality of work of the entire team. Moreover, the involvement in a qualifying training of one of the staff members may create a dynamic within the team, in terms of training. But therefore it is necessary that the team accepts being questioned. Some teams are eager for the effects of their colleague's training, and it is thus much easier to create competence improvement for the entire team. But this is not always the case and the involvement in training of one member is sometimes difficult for her or his peers to accept.

An important practical difficulty is the replacement of the person who is enrolled in the training. Managers refer to the consequences of the absences, linked to the training, notably the recruitment of competent replacing professionals, and ensuring continuity for the children and for the team. The salaried student may feel guilty about leaving when his or her replacement is not assured. On the other hand, a replacement, which ensures the continuity of the work for the team, is experienced as facilitating.

As said, the return in the day care centre, after the training may be difficult for the student, because of his or her development during the training; yet nor is it easy for the team. The salaried student has to regain his or her place, being aware of the effects of the training on the team. Therefore he or she should not impose or dictate changes from what was learned in the training, nor take another place, even if he or she believed that the training required her or him to do other tasks, or to assume a role other than that corresponding to the actual job.

> When I come back, I come back very slowly; I am waiting for the team to come to me.
>
> *(Student)*

These difficulties due to the work-training combination may be increased by problems in team relations. Jealousy may exist, when in the team, a professional was meant to enrol in training and did not do so for different reasons: failing entry, employer's refusal or refusal of funding:

> What we feel is a lot of jealousy. Not always kindness or sympathy. I find there is a lot of frustration. Some persons would want to be in training but do not achieved their goal
>
> *(Trainer)*

The colleague's courage and tenacity in entering training may function as a mirror, reflecting the lack of willingness and ambition of the professionals who did not succeed in entering training, for the reasons referred above. This could create narcissistic wounds, emotional difficulties and be at the origin of conflicting relationships. Rivalry may appear from other educators in the team when they see one of their colleagues, who initially had a much lower level of qualification on entering the job and now turns up with a same level diploma. Moreover, like we see above, if one of the member's training is an opportunity to increase the competences of the entire team, it could also be a source of resistance to changes.

Conditions for success from the team's perspective

The support from the employer is one of the main conditions for success. It guarantees the quality of the replacement of the salaried student. With the different difficulties that the team meets, the support and the coaching are also a condition for success. The team has to be prepared for the effects of the training of one member. When asked what are critical success factors, a manager answers: Preparation and commitment of the team to the training of its colleague. Several moments of discussions, during all the training, are permitting to regulate the potential difficulties.

> The conditions of success? During the team meetings, a time to speak for the salaried student and for the rest of the team to exchange our experiences.
>
> *(Manager)*

> There was time and space for dialogue during the analysis of practices of the team when there were some difficulties.
>
> *(Manager)*

The existence of these times for exchanges that enable the discussion of the effects of the training are mentioned by most of the interviewees. The salaried student should not have a too privileged status:

> It is necessary to remain vigilant when voice is given to all the persons to evocate difficulties. And also to remain cautious not to believe that the student is holding the truth, because he or she has some theoretical courses on training.
>
> *(Educator manager)*

The work on the question of the specific place of each person is fundamental for success. The tutor (an educator in the team) has a crucial role in the learning process but also in the mediation of the relations in the team. The role of tutor was often referred to in the interviews.

> Regular exchanges between the tutor and the student; listening to the difficulties and thinking together about some ways of improvement.
>
> *(Manager)*

> The tutor has a function to ensure the link between the different members of the team and the student: communication and arbitration.
>
> *(Manager)*

Yet, several interviewees evoke the importance of training for the tutor, and the difficulty when it is not available.

> In the training of salaried students, the tutor is not trained. We first meet to explain the content of the course, and we meet again at the end of the course. If no problems occur, this is ok, but when problems occur …
>
> *(Tutor)*

The most salient condition for the success of the training, for the student as well as for the team, is the work upon the disturbances, in the group of analysis of practices. It seems important to deepen the analysis of practices, an essential method to think about in the training processes.

One of the central conclusions of the CoRe report is a systemic view on the competent system: competences are not just an individual challenge but also systemic (Peeters, 2008). This implies that all partners of the educational system are involved in contributing to reflexive positions in initial and in service training, in iterative processes between training and practice and this asks for an interinstitutional steering committee. The French tradition of systemic approaches, in relation to complexity theory (e.g. Morin, 1990; Tricoire, 2002), provides us with three joint influences or movements, when looking at the analysis of practices.

The analysis of practice as pedagogy of alternation between theory and practice

The analysis of practice is a story at the crossroads of three movements in social work and therefore in the early childhood sector. In adult education in the social and educational fields, analyses of practice are welcomed for competence building, for the construction of professional identity and especially for building the reflexive capacity of future professionals.

A first movement

This orientation came from the influence of psychoanalysis and institutional psychotherapy during the 1980s in France. Analysis of practice and supervision in initial and ongoing training were heavily inspired by theoretical psychoanalysis but also by the then popular systemic approach and the sociology of organisations. That inspiration was combined with input from competences development training, from manager training and from scholars in the educational field, such as Fablet (2004).

> Training, by analysing the student's practice, enables him to take position considering all the elements that contribute to the search of the meaning of the action he performs...Which practices do we have to analyse? There are no limits to the field of analysis of the practice. Whether in the clinical, managerial or even in the educational field, any occupational practices can be the topic of an analysis from the authors/actors, with the help of a consultant. This training is based on the alternation, (i.e. within a pedagogic continuity) between the day-care centre and the training centre, between practical experience and theoretical approach. Much more than a pedagogical model, analysis of practices is from our point of view consubstantial with the training process of the reflective practitioner.
>
> *(Dalibert, 2010: p. 8 translation by the authors)*

A second movement

The development of professional training for adults in alternation has also been conceptualised by the CNAM (National Centre for Arts and Crafts). Barbier (2004;

2011) was a significant representative of this movement. The CNAM developed adult training in integrative alternation, according to the 1973 law about continuing education. The pioneers of adult education have put forward the experience as key to the education. Since, this orientation was confirmed and generalised to vocational training, such as work-linked training. Indeed, the use of previous experience and experimentation are an important source of competence development. In a recent perspective, the reference to a social constructivist paradigm in training and education is reflected in the recognition of experience as a process of learning and self-development (Leidner & Jarvenpaa, 1995).

A third movement

This, finally, is represented by the action research especially developed by the EHSS (Ecole des Hautes Etudes en Sciences Sociales). Its director, Henri Desroches, created the cooperative colleges in 1957. The CCRA in Lyon (Cooperative College Rhône-Alpes) belongs to this trend and has worked particularly on training research and especially on social work training. In the training project discussed in this chapter, the CCRA had a significant influence as a result of its expertise in action research. Joel Cadière (1995) and his team accompanied several trainers with this approach and conducted research about the results of this process of training. About the educators of young children, Cadière (2013, translation by the authors) said:

> The EJE bachelors' final works clearly demonstrate reflections on the concrete analysis of professional action related to the care of the young child and taking into account its family.

Five guidelines for the analysis of practices

Based on the writings of previous studies, as well as on our own interviews, there are some guidelines to the successful implementation of this pedagogy.

- The analysis of practice is focused on both personal and professional commitment of the student on his/her way to professional qualification.
- The analysis of practice focuses on the integration of each student in a team and in an organisation. He/she will be stimulated to discuss his/her position in that team and in the organisation and to enhance this position.
- The analysis of practice focuses on the subjective relation of the student with the child and his/her parents and he/she will be stimulated to discuss his/her emotions and his/her professional attitude towards the child and the parents.

The questions asked by students concern first of all the child: his or her development, needs, feelings and emotions. What does the child experience? What does the parent experience? What do I/you feel in this situation? In this context, reason and emotion, analysis and perception cannot be confined to the professional strategy of "keeping at a distance". How does one understand what the child experiences? How then does one construct or exercise professional competence, while being "reasonably involved" in situations (Favre, 2008: pp. 18–19)? One needs to observe the following points:

- The analysis of practice focuses on the methodology of daily pedagogical interventions with children. The students document their daily practice and develop a reflection on their methods, related to the daily action.
- Practice forms the basis of their final work (thesis): collecting situations, identifying issues, research on these issues and proposals for a professional perspective related to the issues analysed in practice. This forms the basis of an attitude of the professional as reflective researcher and of openness to new knowledge.

The analysis of the practice involves different theoretical models: psychoanalysis, social psychology, sociology, organisational analysis and systemic approach. The results remain unpredictable in professional or research terms. Indeed, while the process of analysis of practice is common, the result may be specific for each student. As a consequence, students and trainers need to be ready to work with uncertainty and complexity, and to combine several levels of understanding and intervention.

Conclusion

The different points we explored in this case study illustrate some findings of the CoRe research. First, one of the recommendations in the CoRe report (Urban et al., 2011) is about increasing job mobility. The experience of the present case study suggests that early years staff with low educational qualifications often consist of persons who have encountered serious problems (e.g. socio-economic problems and others) during their school career and have dropped out as a consequence. Yet, the case study also shows that it is possible for them to access a qualifying training at the post-secondary level and to obtain a diploma at a bachelor level. It certainly is a long route and requires a lot of work and commitment, yet every year many professionals have successfully walked that path.

Second, the CoRe report refers to the importance of reflexivity at all levels of the competent system: the individual level, the institutional and inter-institution levels, and the governance level. The report states that at the very core of professional competence lies the constant ability to connect the dimensions of knowledge, practice and values through critical reflection (Urban et al., 2011: p. 35). The case study presented here confirms that reflection is indeed an important condition of success for students and for the team, as well as for the partners who collaborate on such a curriculum.

Like all training, the training for a salaried student is disruptive. It is disruptive for the student, for the changes that occur, compared to previous experiences in the education field, and this is more complex compared to "regular" daytime students.

It involves changes in professional identity, rather than the construction of a professional identity, and this needs to be achieved while continuing to work. It is also disturbing for the team, which can take benefits of the training of one of its members but may resist the propositions of change. The disturbance, in the Piagetian sense (Montangero, 1995), has to be taken in a positive, dynamic way, supporting the student as well as the team to build new competences. For that, a number of conditions need to be respected: student support, qualitative replacement during training sessions, accompanying the team and the tutor. But the main condition is the possibility to reflect on difficulties, questions or even conflicts that are generated by this training experience.

This work about initial and in-service training has resulted in developing personal and professional competencies, reflexivity at individual and collective levels. Inside the group, the development of collective intelligence results in sharing views about the same situation. In the meantime, the experience of this case study has travelled. The analysis of the practice was the subject of a European project on exchanging knowledge on initial training and mentoring between France and Belgium. The project (called Wanda) was developed in 2011–2012. Since then, it has been adapted to the context in the Dutch-speaking community of Belgium and has also become the subject of yet another international project, involving the VBJK (Centre for Innovation in the Early Years) and Artevelde Hogeschool (Higher education center) as well as the International Step by Step Association, a major NGO with representatives in many central and eastern European countries. The approach of analysis of practice has shown its value as a reflexive tool, favouring change and the exchange of practices with partners. As such, it has contributed to the construction of novel practices.

References

Barbier, J.-M. & Galatanu, O. (2004). *Les savoirs d'action, une mise en mot des compétences?* Paris: L'Harmattan.

Barbier, J.-M. (2011). *Vocabulaire d'analyse des activités.* Paris: L'Harmattan.

Cadière, J. (1995). Etude des trajectoires professionnelles et sociales des éducateurs de jeunes enfants issus des formations par contrat de qualification. Unpublished document.

Cadière, J. (2013). *L'apprentissage de la recherche en travail social.* Rennes: Presses de l'Ecole des Hautes Etudes en Santé Publique.

Dalibert, C. (2010). *L'analyse de la pratique, revisiter les méthodes, questionner les évidences: dossier n°140.* Lyon: CREAI Rhône-Alpes.

Fablet, D., Favre, D., Malleval, D. & Pueyo, B. (2004). *Professionnels de la petite enfance et analyse de la pratique.* Paris: L'Harmattan.

Favre, D. (2008). Un praticien-réflexif dans une mise à l'épreuve entre affect et responsabilité (balance between affect and responsability). *Children in Europe – Le Furet,* 28, pp. 18–19.

Leidner, D. E. & Jarvenpaa, S. L. (1995). The use of information technology to enhance management school education: A theoretical view. *MIS Quarterly,* 19, p. 3.

Ministère de l'emploi et de la solidarité (2000). *Décret d'août 2000.* Paris: Author.

Montangero, J. (1995). *Piaget ou l'intelligence en marche.* Brussels: Mardaga.

Mony, M. (2002). Mal de mère et pied marin. In P. Bensoussan (ed.). *Petite enfance et culture en mouvement*. Toulouse: Erès, pp. 71–90.

Mony, M. (2013). Parcours de qualification professionnelle de salaries: c'est possible et efficace! *Le Furet*, 72, pp. 22–24.

Mony, M. (2013). Formation et métier s'enrichissent continuellement: 40 ans de diplôme d'EJE. *La gazette des collectifs- enfants- parents–professionnels*, 109, pp. 6–9.

Morin, M. (1990). *Introduction à la pensée complexe*. Paris: Seuil.

Peeters, J. & Vandenbroeck, M. (2012). A la recherche des systèmes compétents: conclusions et recommandations de CoRe: un projet de recherche européen sur les compétences requises en EAPE. *Petite Enfance*, 107, pp. 79–86.

Pueyo, B. (2004). Rapport final du groupe de travail Accompagner le développement de l'accès aux formations en cours d'emploi. Unpublished document.

Thollon Behar, M. P. (2013) Se former tout en étant salarié. *Le Furet*, 72, pp. 14–16.

Tricoire, B. (2002). *Le génie du tiers*. Paris: l'Harmattan.

Urban, M., Vandenbroeck, M., Lazzari, A., Peeters, J. & Van Laere, K. (2011). *Competence requirements for early childhood education and care*. London and Ghent: UEL and UGent.

Vandenbroeck, M. (2011) Pour une approche systémique de la formation des professionnels. In *Bien être des jeunes enfants dans l'accueil et l'éducation en France et ailleurs*, Actes du colloque, DREES, 10.

3

CONTINUOUS PROFESSIONAL SUPPORT AND QUALITY

The case of Pistoia

Tullia Musatti, Mariacristina Picchio and Susanna Mayer

This chapter describes the actions through which the Municipality of Pistoia, Italy, has implemented a substantial and continuous investment in sustaining the quality of early childhood education and care (ECEC) services. The case of Pistoia is a prime example of how the municipal governance of a system of ECEC services can supply quantitatively consistent ECEC provision while ensuring its good quality. We will argue that professionalism is a key element of the quality of Italian municipal ECEC and highlight how continuous professional support contributes to develop it and makes it a major dimension in a competent ECEC system.

First, we will provide some data on ECEC in Italy and outline the relevance of the municipal provision as well as the essential features of municipal ECEC professionalism. Then, we will draft a brief history of the development of ECEC in Pistoia and analyse the main elements that characterise professionalism in ECEC and ensure its quality. Finally, we will describe the procedures for the documentation and analysis of educational practice that have been developed during some action-research initiatives in Pistoia and discuss their potential and future implementation in other contexts.

ECEC in Italy and the role of the municipalities

Italy has a split ECEC system according to children's ages (UNESCO, 2010). Only 12.2% of children under three years old attend a *nido*, that is a group day care centre, and a further 1.7% attend other services such as family day care (ISTAT, 2014), whereas about 95% of three to six year olds attend *scuola dell'infanzia* mostly from 8–8.30 a.m. until 4–4.30 p.m.

Services for under threes employ two types of practitioners: the *educatori* (educators), who work with the children, and the *addetti ai servizi generali* or *ausiliari* (assistants), whose tasks are to clean and arrange the environment, take care of the play materials (together with the educators) and help to prepare meals and distribute food. For the *educatore*, an upper-secondary school degree in educational studies (ISCED-3) is required. However, most recent regional laws either prefer or require a university degree, and some universities have designed a specific BA programme (ISCED-4) in Early Education. The practitioner who works with children in the *scuola dell'infanzia* is called *insegnante* (teacher) and, since 1998, a university degree in *Scienze della Formazione Primaria*, (ISCED-5), which diploma qualifies the status of the pre-primary or primary teacher, is required.

Although, in both sectors, most of the services are supported by public financing or are provided by public institutions, different levels of public administration are involved in their governance. The regional administrations have exclusive competence to make regulations on all the services for under threes, while municipalities are responsible for their local governance and run or fund (totally or partially) the great majority (more than 80%) of these services.

The *scuola dell'infanzia* is under the responsibility of the national government, which also provides the majority of these services, while only a small number of them are provided by municipalities. However, the relevance of the municipal investment in early childhood education goes beyond the national percentage (9%) of children enrolled in municipal *scuole dell'infanzia*. Actually these services are distributed unequally over regions and are quite numerous in larger cities (Bologna, Florence, Milan, Naples, Palermo, Rome, Turin) and in middle-sized cities in the Central and Northern regions, where they were set up during the post-war period and maintained also when the State took on the responsibility of pre-primary education in 1968. In the early 70s, when a national Act assigned the responsibility for the creation of *nido* services for children under three to the regional and local governments, the cities that had already invested in *scuole dell'infanzia* integrated the childcare centres into the Education sector. This integration allowed more coherent policies regarding early education and the development of an educational culture shared by *scuola dell'infanzia* and *nido*, despite the differences in regulations, organisations, access procedures and the professional status of practitioners.

Over the years, the cities have developed quite different policies and educational approaches in accordance with local cultures and political orientations. In the cities that made major investments, we find not only an important increase in the provision of ECEC, but also experimentation with new types of services and some services of excellence, which have been internationally acknowledged, as in Reggio Emilia (Rinaldi, 2005). The creation of formal and informal networks among these cities allowed the development of a set of organisational and cultural features, which have had an important role in shaping ECEC systems in other cities.

Almost all municipal ECEC services are inspired by a participatory approach. The *Gruppo educativo* (educational group) of the *nido* or *scuola dell'infanzia* is composed by both *educatori/insegnanti* and *ausiliari*, who cooperate and integrate their different competences into a global professional performance. With this regard it is noteworthy that many municipal regulations provide a detailed description of the professional identity of the service as a whole, whereas they do not define the professional competences of each type of personnel. A participatory approach also inspires the relationships between children's families and ECEC services. A great deal of attention has been given to the establishment of good relationships between parents and staff and to parents' involvement in the daily life of the services. Decision-making committees, with parents and representatives of the staff, are promoted and regulated by formal acts. In the Italian ECEC tradition, the concept of participation "encompasses both civic engagement and its expression in [an] organised form of participation and control – the so called *gestione sociale*" (Mantovani, 2007, p. 1106). As Malaguzzi pointed out "… the experience of *gestione sociale* … should be expanded into a model of active and responsible participation at any political and administrative level … in our cities" (Malaguzzi, 1972, p. 142).

Municipal ECEC experiences are also characterised by the explicit attention given to continuous professional development. Municipal ECEC practitioners, both *educatori* and *insegnanti*, benefit from a number of paid hours in addition to those spent with children. These hours must be spent in planning educational activities, meeting with parents, and participating in in-service training. Over the years, in-service training initiatives have represented an important opportunity to increase professionalism of ECEC staff (Mantovani, 2001), and they have become a place for the development of an important cultural elaboration of the issues related to early childhood education on a local basis (Lazzari, Picchio & Musatti, 2013). Their most peculiar characteristic is that they are situated, in the double sense that they are under the influence of the local culture – for example, as it will be described in the following, in Pistoia the great aesthetic sensibility led to specific training initiatives on the aesthetic features of ECEC environment, and that they are referred to the analysis of actual processes observed in the service. As most of these initiatives are organised on a group basis and involve all of the practitioners in the service, they contribute to the development of a collective set of competences and knowledge, and they reinforce the collegiality of the professional work and the cultural identity of each service.

The function of pedagogical coordination is a further important quality element of the municipal ECEC, in which the collective responsibility of *educatori* or *insegnanti*, as a group, is valued and no director or leader is present in the service. This function, which consists of supporting educational practices in the services, promoting and organising in-service training, favouring networking among services in the city, mediating between educational services and municipal administration, is served by a team of qualified professionals, named *coordinatori pedagogici* or *pedagogisti* (pedagogical coordinator), with pedagogic and psychological competences and management responsibilities. Each pedagogical coordinator is in charge of a number of services and participates in municipal or inter-city teams of coordination (Baudelot et al., 2003; Musatti & Mayer, 2003). Although the competence profile of pedagogical coordinators is not defined at the national level, the relevance of their role in supporting the quality of ECEC services and in integrating their programme within a larger cultural perspective is widely recognised (Catarsi, 2010). Pedagogical coordinators are found in most cities and the presence of a pedagogical coordinator is one of the basic requirements for private services if they wish to receive public funding.

At the present time, the municipal ECEC is facing old and new challenges, which can have important implications for its quality.

The split system at national level between services for under threes, which are still considered as socio-educational services and are regulated locally, and the *scuola dell'infanzia*, which are included in the national educational system, as well as the gap between the level of initial training and the professional status of *educatori* and *insegnanti*, are echoed at municipal level; however, there is a broad consensus that an integrated educational system should be ensured from birth to age six (the age of compulsory schooling).

The impact of the financial crisis on the municipal expenditures have hampered the development of ECEC provision for the under threes. Under the pressure of the growing demands of parents, municipal administrations have integrated private services into their ECEC systems provided that they comply with some qualification requirements (the presence of pedagogical coordinators, paid hours for in-service training, networking within the municipal provision), ensure equitable accessibility, and accept systematic evaluation by the municipal pedagogical coordinators.

In recent years, another important challenge is emerging with regard to the maintenance of an educational culture of good quality in municipal services. Because most of the municipal *scuole dell'infanzia* and *nido* services were opened in the 1970s, an increasing number of experienced *educatori* who participated actively to the ECEC culture and educational practice are retiring or will retire in the next few years. How to ensure the transmission and further development of the educational culture that has grown inside the services and has become rooted in their practices is an issue under discussion in many cities, and specific procedures for this cultural transmission within the services have been the subject of experimentation.

The story of municipal ECEC provision in Pistoia is inscribed within this framework.

The development of municipal ECEC system in Pistoia

Pistoia is a city of about 90,000 inhabitants in Tuscany. An ancient Etrurian settlement and a Roman colony, during the Grand Duchy of the Medicis in the fourteenth century, it was an important political and cultural city. Civil and religious monuments in the Romanesque, Renaissance and Baroque styles embellish the city, which has a vibrant cultural life. In the last seventy years, Pistoia has been constantly governed by left wing or centre-left wing political parties and has benefited from a stable social and political context, which has been characterised by a strong commitment to ECEC.

In 1968, when a national act created the state public preschool in Italy, many municipal classrooms of *scuola dell'infanzia* were already functioning in Pistoia. During the early 1970s, the number of both municipal *scuole dell'infanzia* and *nido* increased. Since 1987, the ECEC system has been enriched by *Spazio Gioco* (playgroups) for 18 to 36 month-old children for two or three half-days per week and by a Centre for children and parents (Galardini, Giovannini & Musatti, 1993; Mantovani & Musatti, 1996).

In 2015, the Pistoia municipality operates ten *nido* and other services that reach 24.8% of children under three years old and eleven *scuole dell'infanzia* that cater to 37% of three to six-year-old children, and four thematic workshops (*AreaBambini*). Eight private *nido* bring the overall coverage to 33% of children under three years old in the city, while fifteen more *scuola dell'infanzia* are run by the state and eight are run privately, reaching more than 90% of children aged three to six.

The municipal administration has enabled increasing homogeneity in the working conditions and salaries of educational staff of *nido* and *scuola dell'infanzia*, and all of them are called teachers. In 2015, the municipal ECEC system employs a total of 188 staff (119 teachers, 52 assistants and 17 cooks).

The quantitative development of the ECEC system has been accompanied by a major investment in its quality. In the early 70s, two pedagogical consultants with managerial responsibilities were already employed by the municipality in permanent fulltime positions, and, some years later, the responsibility for services for children under three years old was shifted from the Department of Social Welfare to the Department of Education (together with *scuole dell'infanzia*), and a team of pedagogical coordination was formed.

Furthermore, since the early 70s the municipal administration has been making a major investment in the professionalisation of ECEC practitioners by organising systematic in-service training initiatives. In-service training is a right and a duty for both the municipal administration and the teachers, who have 150 paid non-contact hours per year and the formal commitment to provide in-service training to practitioners is stated by the City of Pistoia Chart of ECEC Services. Most of in-service training initiatives are organised on a group basis and involve all of the practitioners working in the service. Over the years, they have been focused on very different themes: child development and care, children's and families' needs, or other sociological and anthropological themes, in accordance with the idea that ECEC professionalism should be based on a wide cultural formation that crosses the borders of the traditional sciences of education (Galardini, 2010). Most of the in-service training initiatives have involved the practitioners in observation and documentation activities, as they were embedded in action-research projects in collaboration with research agencies such as ISTC-CNR, the University of Pavia, and the University of Florence.

In order to support the implementation of a coherent pedagogical project, the municipality has provided a variety of opportunities for professional exchange between the practitioners of all of the ECEC services in the city and has involved them in programmes directed toward all of the children in the city, such as children's play events in the central squares of the city, storytelling sessions in the streets, and so on.

Practitioners have constantly been engaged in professional exchanges with other Italian cities, whose ECEC services are of high quality, such as Reggio Emilia, the association *Gruppo Nazionale Nidi e Infanzia*, which was hosted by Pistoia municipality for its second national meeting in 1982 (AA.VV., 1983), and ECEC practitioners from Denmark, Belgium, France, Spain and Switzerland. Over the years, Pistoia has received more and more visits from well-known international scholars, such as Urie Bronfenbrenner, Carolyn Pope-Edwards, Hermine Sinclair and Mira Stambak, and it has had opportunities for fruitful interactions with research agencies and universities outside of Italy, such as Université de Paris XIII, CRESAS-INRP and IEDPE in France, University of Massachusetts and Smith College in the USA, Jumonji University in Japan, Association Rosa Sensat and Universitat de les Illes Balears in Spain, University of Edinburgh and Centre for Literacy in Primary Education in the United Kingdom, Université de Liège, Universiteit Gent and VBJK in Belgium.

Furthermore, Pistoia has hosted teams of ECEC practitioners from other Italian and European cities, opening its services to their visits, enquiries and discussion during long-lasting formative initiatives (Ben Soussan, 2008; Die & Hurtig, 2015). In the years 1997–2000, Pistoia underwent a formal twinning with Palermo, Sicily, hosted groups of Palermo *nido* practitioners (a total of 150), and provided them with specific in-service training initiatives, both in Pistoia and in Palermo (Galardini et al., 1997). This experience, which has resulted in the improvement of the quality of *nido* provision in Palermo, was useful also to Pistoia teachers, who acknowledged the importance of an external view of their practices, as well as the importance of being able to articulate their own practices (Romano et al., 2001). A similar experience was provided to several groups of *nido* practitioners from Rome (Terzi, 2006).

The main elements of Pistoia ECEC quality

The attention to ECEC quality results also from the constant commitment of the municipal administration to elaborate a coherent general pedagogical framework in which the variety of educational projects implemented by the services, as well as other interventions and actions directed to children in the city, should be inscribed. This commitment emerges also in the Chart of Pistoia ECEC services, which asserts that all services refer to a coherent pedagogical framework, albeit "it does not originate from a a priori defined theory but it is based on the educational practice and is continuously elaborated by all professionals in the services". The core is a notion of *educare* as providing support to children's growth and development rather than teaching or transmitting knowledge to them. Consequently, educational projects should be centred on children's inclination to explore, learn and socialise, with a special emphasis on socialisation among peers, in the adult-peer group in the school, and in the city, and on the praxical dimension of learning. As children's wishes and needs change according to social and cultural changes and contexts, no educational model can be predetermined, though some general features characterise the implementation of this city pedagogical framework in the various services.

First of all, a great value is assigned to the daily experience made by children in the services rather than to specific opportunities of learning. The underlying idea is that ECEC context is an important "place of the daily life" for the children, whose social and cognitive processes develop mainly within a continuous interaction with their daily life environment. Consequently, a great deal of attention is paid to all the dimensions (physical, symbolic and social aspects) of the ECEC environment.

A major objective is to establish stable and positive interpersonal relationships between all actors: between children, between children and teachers, between teachers and parents, as well as between teachers and the pedagogical coordinators. Both in *nido* and *scuola dell'infanzia* intense relationships between children and teachers can be established over the years, as the same group of teachers is responsible of the same group of children during their three years' attendance. A strong partnership between teachers and children's families is also pursued (Galardini & Giovannini, 2001; Sharmahd & Terlizzi, 2008), as well as with the whole urban community. Likewise, the municipal management and the coordination team give a great deal of attention to their own relationships with all practitioners in the services.

The emphasis on providing a friendly and pleasant context is mirrored in the attentive care and arrangement of the physical setting (space organisation, furniture and play materials) in order to ensure children's well-being, support their autonomous exploration, play and interactions, as well as to ensure the comfort of adults (practitioners and parents). This high attention to the quality of environment is related to a broad sensibility to the aesthetic dimension of children's and adults' experience in ECEC services (AA.VV., 1999), so much that Pistoia educational approach has been defined as "a pedagogy of good taste" (Becchi, 2010; Becchi & Bondioli, 1997).

This general approach to early childhood education has inspired municipal policies and has had important effects on ECEC professionalism.

A general willingness to engage in social interaction permeates Pistoia practitioners' attitudes and behaviour, and results in their high responsiveness to children's needs and demands, and their commitment to understanding children's social, emotional and cognitive experiences (Musatti & Mayer, 2001). Similar attitudes emerge in practitioners' interactions with parents. Since the first entry of each child and parent into the service, practitioners act as welcoming hosts at a common home. The increasing familiarity of parents with the service and its practitioners transforms this attitude into more a more intense relationship. This hospitable attitude has been explicitly adopted as a characteristic of Pistoia services in welcoming visitors, practitioners from other cities, students and researchers.

Another feature that characterises Pistoia professionalism is *collegiality*. As we have said, teachers are contemporarily present in the classroom for a certain amount of their working time and share the responsibility for the same group of children; moreover, they have a variety of opportunities for sharing perspectives and engaging in discussions together, such as regular group meetings at different levels (classroom, service or more services) and in-service training initiatives. Over the years, these conditions have supported practitioners' shared understanding of children's needs and potential and planning of innovative practices. The development of the *collegial* dimension of educational practice has also been promoted by a strong feeling of belonging to an innovative social experience, which has characterised the history of Italian municipal ECEC. However, in Pistoia's experience, the focus on *collegiality* has not prevented the promotion of the specific professional preferences or competences of individual practitioners, whose abilities in arts crafting, science education, storytelling or music have been encouraged and made available to all other practitioners (Galardini, 1995).

The last, but not least, feature of Pistoia professionalism is the teachers' heightened reflexivity, which emerges from their continuous analysis of educational practice. The teachers' reflexivity is sustained by a well-developed discursive competence which seems to be shared by almost all of Pistoia practitioners (Becchi, 2010) and may result from frequent group discussions during in-service initiatives, as well from the local traditional competence in the use of oral language. It is also nourished by the practices of observation and documentation, as most of the teachers are used to observing and documenting children's behaviour and activities during the daily life in the service. Thus, documentation accompanies educational processes by making daily life in the service visible for the children and their parents and promoting the children's knowledge and shared memories, as well as the parents' involvement. Through documentation, teachers are induced to continuously analyse their practice in order to understand its meaning and implications and, eventually, to change it. From this perspective, documentation is considered as a product as well as a driving force of practitioners' reflection on their practices (Galardini, 2009; 2010) and its use has been strongly supported by the pedagogical coordination team. In Pistoia, documentation is realised in various ways: simple written notes on a play episode or on children's behaviour or interactions, photos of social events in the service or of specific play activities, and the individual journal of each child's journey across her three years of attendance at the *nido*. The teachers also pay particular attention to the formal and aesthetic aspects of documentation (Giovannini, 2001; Magrini & Gandini, 2001).

New challenges and further development of Pistoia ECEC professionalism

Over the last decade, a significant turnover of practitioners has occurred in the Pistoia municipal *nido*, as many teachers have retired or moved to the *scuola dell'infanzia*. Almost 50% of *nido* teachers have been newly employed during that period; most of them have a university degree, albeit poor preparation in early childhood education. Most importantly, major problems have emerged regarding how to ensure cultural cohesion in the educational groups and continuity in the city's educational project.

In 2006, our research group at ISTC-CNR, which has engaged in long-term cooperation with Pistoia municipal ECEC, was committed to identifying new strategies in order to support practitioners during this change. Thus, an action-research project was developed in close cooperation with the team of pedagogical coordinators, which was aimed at identifying new documentation procedures that could be continuously accomplished by *nido* teachers and could support their *collegial* reflection on their practices. As a first step, the project was conducted by a team composed of one pedagogical coordinator, seven *nido* teachers and five researchers, who met periodically over three educational years and presented their elaborations to all municipal *nido* personnel at the end of each year. The project fitted naturally into a preceding procedure of documentation. In a study conducted a few years before by the ISTC-CNR and the teachers of *nido Lagomago* (Musatti et al., 2014) on children's social and cognitive processes during their everyday life in the *nido*, videos were registered weekly over two academic years and integrated by written ethnographic notes, in which the teachers reported brief descriptions of the children's experience during the week. Eventually, the weekly report was also considered to be a useful tool of documentation by other *nido* teachers, and the habit of writing such weekly reports spread spontaneously throughout the city.

The project faced some challenges. A first practical question – "What to do with all the weekly reports we are writing?" – led to new procedures for the documentation and analysis of the evolution of children's experience over the year. Further questions – including "What is the goal of the weekly reports?" and "Why are so many teachers motivated to write them?" – led us to analyse the meaning of documentation, its relation to evaluation, and the function of both of them in educational practice.

The weekly reports had some specific features that distinguished them from other forms of documentation currently practised in Pistoia ECEC.

As we described above, Pistoia teachers' high reflexive competence was exercised mostly through oral communication. Although some written notes were usually included in the documentation produced, they consisted mostly of brief punctual descriptions of children's activities or events. In the weekly reports, a more thorough use of writing was required. In the weekly reports, the teachers were requested to write a short *narrative* (Bruner, 1996), which would represent the daily experience shared by children and teachers and outline the meaning of the social, emotional and cognitive processes involved in it, as well as the relations between successive events.

Writing these reports was a *collegial* commitment. At the end of the week, the teachers in charge of each group of children had to find the time to meet together (during their supplementary hours or even during children's naptime), adopt some distance from their own personal experiences, discuss the experience made by children during the week, decide what to write, and, eventually, plan future actions.

The reports could also convey a meaningful representation of the daily life in the *nido* to other stakeholders, such as parents, pedagogical coordinators and decision makers, enhancing democratic participation in educational choices. In fact, when teachers decided to display their reports, the parents greatly appreciated reading them and their involvement in sharing the educational commitment with the teachers increased.

The analysis of the weekly reports encouraged the practitioners to evaluate their practices in order to monitor and eventually improve them. It also implied a further focusing on the ultimate significance of evaluation. Teachers acknowledged that they all shared a basic implicit educational project, including major goals and minor objectives with regard to each age group of children, and that they should evaluate whether these objectives had been reached on the basis of the analysis of children's experience, which had been documented in the reports. As these results can be appreciated only over a period longer than a week, they decided to carry out an overall analysis of the sequence of the weekly reports over four-five months, as this was considered to be a meaningful period in the children's lives in the *nido*. This second-level analysis was discussed during meetings of the entire service (or more services together) with pedagogical coordinators in order to evaluate whether the evolution of children's experience was moving towards the educational objectives pursued. The focus on children's everyday experience enhanced the value assigned to the ordinary aspects of life in the educational context, rather than to specific learning or play activities. The analysis of the children's experience over different periods highlighted the process of its development and the impact of educational practice on it.

At the end of the three years, the procedures were used by most of the teachers of the municipal Pistoia *nido*, and their sustainability during the current educational practice had been assessed (Picchio et al., 2012). In the following years, during a further action-research project with the ISTC-CNR research group, the written documentation initiative underwent some development. First, the processes of *collegiality* among practitioners and networking between services in the city were reinforced, as the use of weekly reports was extended to all municipal *nido* teachers, and more sustainable procedures were validated for their periodical analysis in *collegial* meetings of the whole *nido* group or between small groups of teachers who care for same-aged children in various *nido* and pedagogical coordinators. In the last year, a parallel initiative has also been launched within two *scuole dell'infanzia*, and, in the framework of an overall re-organisation of the municipal governance of ECEC system, private *nido* personnel were also included within the current in-service training initiatives organised by the municipality, and began using the weekly reports.

A second important innovation was the integration of photos and written reports in order to carry out an in-depth analysis of the evolution of specific aspects of children's experience. Such a mixed documentation allows teachers' to expand their narratives on children's experience and to better share also its affective dimension with other colleagues in more extended *collegial* meetings.

In sum, the procedures for written documentation provided the practitioners with a stable framework to exercise reflexivity within *collegial* contexts. As the procedures encouraged the practitioners to discuss their educational goals and objectives, they outlined the crucial role of pedagogical coordinators and sustained the dialogue between the older and newer generations of practitioners about the city's pedagogical framework. The collaboration with a team of researchers within a participative action-research project endorsed practitioners' agency (Peeters & Vandenbroeck, 2011). Through the use of documentation procedures, the dimension of evaluation, which is inherent in all initiatives of reflexivity but is often concealed, became evident and explicit through discussions, and its usefulness for innovating and improving the practices was confirmed (Picchio, Di Giandomenico & Musatti, 2014).

Concluding remarks

In Pistoia, as in many other Italian cities, ECEC has been conceived as a major investment by the city in order to meet families' needs and ensure children's right to early education. We have described how, over more than 40 years, the municipal administration has given special attention to the realisation of an ECEC system of good quality and many services of excellence in the city.

A particular social and cultural climate, which has characterised the development of municipal ECEC in Pistoia as in many other Italian cities, has been supported by dynamic municipal management. In particular, we have highlighted how continuous pedagogical support to ECEC practitioners has been one of the basic elements on which a good quality ECEC system has been grounded. It has allowed practitioners to go beyond their initial poor competences in early education, as it has been described in other contexts (Peeters & Sharmahd, 2014), and was the centrepiece of the construction of a competent ECEC system (Urban et al., 2012). The collaborative and democratic culture that inspires the system in Pistoia has played the most important role in tackling the tensions due to the Italian ECEC split system (Oberhümer, 2005), dealing with generational changes and surviving economic difficulties.

As we have described, continuous professional development has been realised by specific conditions:

- time for shared reflexivity in the group of practitioners, which is guaranteed by a number of paid non-contact hours to be spent in planning, discussing, and analysing practices;
- an organised framework of in-service training provided by the municipal administration in which the practitioners' reflexivity could also be nourished by expert contributions on broad cultural themes;
- a pedagogical coordination team that accompanies (Pirard, 2011) practitioners in their commitment to continuous improvement.

A recent study conducted by the European Foundation for the Improvement of Living and Working (Peeters et al., 2014) has outlined the same conditions as crucial ingredients for continuous professional development initiatives that are effective in enhancing the quality of ECEC services.

We have shown that the high level of ECEC professionalism in Pistoia mostly consists of a general willingness to engage in social interaction with children and parents, and a high degree of reflexivity in analysing children's experience and in questioning educational practice. These dimensions of professionalism, which are acknowledged as basic competences and qualities of any care work (Cameron & Moss, 2007), are practised in participatory contexts and are enhanced by *collegiality*. We have also highlighted how documentation has become a usual and common practice in all ECEC services and has reinforced practitioners' processes of reflexivity and their sharing in collegial meetings. Our analysis of the action-research initiative recently conducted in collaboration with our research group has shown that it is possible to elaborate procedures for the documentation, analysis and evaluation of the educational practice to be used in current professional practice and to provide further support to processes of reflexivity and their sharing.

References

AA.VV. (1983). *Il bambino di fronte ad una famiglia e ad una società che cambiano: atti del convegno nazionale sugli Asili nido, Pistoia, 25–28/03/1982*. Bergamo: Juvenilia.

AA.VV. (1999). *L'immaginario bambino: le esperienze educative del Comune di Pistoia nei disegni e nella grafica di Andrea Rauch, 1979–1999* [The imaginary world of the child]. Bergamo: Edizioni Junior (Dual language Italian and English edition).

Baudelot, O., Rayna, S., Mayer, S. & Musatti, T. (2003). A comparative analysis of the function of coordination of early childhood education and care in France and Italy. *Early Years Education, 11*, 105–116.

Becchi, E. (2010). *Una pedagogia del buon gusto*. Milan: FrancoAngeli.

Becchi, E., & Bondioli, A. (Eds) (1997). *Valutare e valutarsi nelle scuole dell'infanzia del Comune di Pistoia: un modello di formazione degli insegnanti*. Bergamo: Edizioni Junior.

Ben Soussan, P. (2008). Il faut ouvrir des écoles maternelles comme à Pistoia. *Spirale, 46*, 2, 7–11.

Bruner, J. (1996). *The Culture of Education*. Cambridge: Harvard University Press.

Cameron, C., & Moss, P. (2007). *Care Work in Europe: Current understandings and future directions*. London and New York: Routledge.

Catarsi, E. (Ed.) (2010). *Coordinamento pedagogico e servizi per l'infanzia*. Bergamo: Edizioni Junior.

Die, N., & Hurtig, M.H. (2015). Pistoia... Gap... et le réseau 'Devenir d'enfance'. In S. Rayna, C. Bouve, & P. Moisset (Eds), *Un curriculum pour un acceuil de qualité de la petite enfance* (pp. 175–188). Toulouse: Érès.

Galardini, A.L. (1995). Le scuole dell'infanzia comunali a Pistoia. In E. Becchi (Ed.), *Manuale della Scuola del bambino dai tre ai sei anni* (pp. 119–127). Milan: FrancoAngeli.

Galardini, A.L. (2009). Réseau et documentation: l'expérience italienne pour la qualité éducative. In S. Rayna, C. Bouve, & P. Moisset (Eds), *Pour un accueil de qualité de la petite enfance: quel curriculum?* (pp. 79–86). Toulouse: Édition Érès.

Galardini, A.L. (2010). Intrecci con la comunità. In E. Becchi, *Una pedagogia del buon gusto* (pp. 11–37). Milan: FrancoAngeli.

Galardini, A.L., & Giovannini, D. (2001). Pistoia: creating a dynamic, open system to serve children, families and community. In L. Gandini & C. Pope Edwards (Eds), *Bambini:*

The Italian approach to infant/toddler care (pp. 89–104). New York (NY): Teachers College Press.

Galardini, A.L., Giovannini, D., Mandalà, M., & Tonucci, F. (1997). Famiglie e città. Palermo e Pistoia si incontrano. *Bambini a Palermo*, supplement to *Bambini, XIII, 6*, 1–24.

Galardini, A. L., Giovannini, D., & Musatti, T. (Eds) (1993). AreaBambini: i nuovi servizi educativi per l'infanzia a Pistoia. *Bambini, 1*, 1–32.

Giovannini, D. (2001). Traces of childhood: a child's diary. In L. Gandini & C. Pope Edwards (Eds), *Bambini: the Italian approach to infant/toddler care* (pp. 146–151). New York (NY): Teachers College Press.

ISTAT (2014). L'offerta comunale di asili nido e altri servizi socio-educativi per la prima infanzia. Anno scolastico 2012/2013. *Statistiche Report*, 24 July 2014.

Lazzari, A., Picchio, M., & Musatti, T. (2013). Sustaining ECEC quality through continuing professional development: systemic approaches to practitioners' professionalisation in the Italian context. *Early Years: An International Research Journal, 33, 2*, 133–145.

Magrini, G., & Gandini, L. (2001). Inclusion: Dario's story. In L. Gandini & C. Pope Edwards (Eds), *Bambini: The Italian approach to infant/toddler care* (pp. 152–163). New York (NY): Teachers College Press.

Malaguzzi, L. (1972). La nuova socialità del bambino e dell'insegnante attraverso l'esperienza della gestione sociale nella scuola dell'infanzia. In AA. VV. (1972), *La gestione sociale nella scuola dell'infanzia* (pp. 139–152). Rome: Editori Riuniti.

Mantovani, S. (2001). Infant-toddler centers in Italy today: tradition and innovation. In L. Gandini & C. Pope Edwards (Eds), *Bambini: The Italian approach to infant/toddler Care* (pp. 23–37). New York (NY): Teachers College Press.

Mantovani, S. (2007). Early childhood education in Italy. In R.S. New & M. Cochran, *Early childhood education: An international encyclopedia* Vol. 4 (pp. 1110–1115). Westport (CT): Praeger Publishers.

Mantovani, S. & Musatti, T. (1996). New educational provisions for young children in Italy. *European Journal of Psychology of Education, 11*, 119–128.

Musatti, T., Giovannini, D., Mayer, S. & Group Nido Lagomago (2014). How to construct a curriculum in an Italian *nido*. In L. Miller & C. Cameron (Eds), *International perspectives in the early years* (pp. 85–110). London: Sage.

Musatti, T., & Mayer, S. (2001). Knowing and learning in an educational context: A study in the infant-toddler centres of the city of Pistoia. In L. Gandini & C. Pope Edwards (Eds), *Bambini: The Italian approach to infant/toddler care* (pp. 167–180). New York (NY): Teachers College Press.

Musatti, T., & Mayer, S. (Eds) (2003). *Il coordinamento dei servizi educativi per l'infanzia: una funzione emergente in Italia e in Europa*. Bergamo: Edizioni Junior.

Oberhümer, P. (2005). Conceptualising the early childhood pedagogue: policy approaches and issues of professionalism. *European Early Childhood Research Journal, 13, 1*, 5–16.

Peeters, J., Budginaite, I., Cameron, C., Hauari, H., Lazzari, A., Peleman. B., & Siarova, H. (2014). *Impact of continuous professional development and working conditions of early childhood education and care practitioners on quality, staff-child-interactions and children's outcomes: A systematic synthesis of research evidence*. Ghent: VBJK.

Peeters, J., & Sharmahd, N. (2014). Professional development for ECEC practitioners with responsibilities for children at risk: which competences and in-service training are needed? *European Early Childhood Research Journal, 22, 3*, 412–424, DOI: 10.1080/1350293X.2014.912903.

Peeters, J., & Vandenbroeck, M. (2011). Child care practitioners and the process of professionalization. In L. Miller & C. Cable (Eds), *Professionalization, leadership and management in the early years* (pp. 62–76). London: Sage.

Picchio, M., Di Giandomenico, I., & Musatti, T. (2014). The use of documentation in a participatory system of evaluation. *Early Years: An International Research Journal, 34,* 2, 133–145.

Picchio, M., Giovannini, D., Mayer, S., & Musatti, T. (2012). Documentation and analysis of children's experience: an ongoing collegial activity for early childhood professionals. *Early Years: An International Research Journal, 32,* 2, 159–170.

Pirard, F. (2011). From the curriculum framework to its dissemination: the accompaniment of educational practices in care facilities for children under three years. *European Early Childhood Education Journal, 19,* 2, 255–268.

Rinaldi, C. (2005). *In Dialogue with Reggio Emilia: Listening, researching and learning.* London: Routledge.

Romano, L., Piazzese, P., & Parisi, D. (2001). Esperienza del Progetto Leonardo a Palermo: Séminaire Leonardo Da Vinci Program, 1999–2001, F/98/1/64041/PI/III.3.a/FPC, Paris, May 2001.

Sharmahd, N., & Terlizzi, T. (2008). *Contesto e relazioni: educatrici e genitori nei nidi pistoiesi.* Bergamo: Edizioni Junior.

Terzi, N. (Ed.) (2006). *Prospettive di qualità al nido: il ruolo del coordinatore educativo.* Bergamo: Edizioni Junior.

UNESCO (2010). *Caring and learning together: A cross-national study on the integration of ECEC within education.* Paris: UNESCO.

Urban, M., Vandenbroeck, M., Van Laere, K. Lazzari, A., & Peeters, J. (2012). Towards competent systems in early childhood education and care: implications for policy and practice. *European Journal of Education, 47,* 4, 508–526.

4

THE COMPETENT EARLY CHILDHOOD EDUCATION AND CARE SYSTEM IN THE CITY OF GHENT

A long-term investment in continuous professional development

Jan Peeters, Chris De Kimpe and Steven Brandt

Introduction

Childcare in the city of Ghent has a long history and has been extensively documented by reports, articles and videos since the end of the 1970s (Peeters, 1993; Peeters, 2008; UNESCO, 2010; De Meyer, 2012). In 1979, before any Continuing Professional Development (CPD) initiatives were taken, a baseline quality measurement was carried out. Later studies on the impact of the CPD initiatives on the quality of the services were set up in 1982 and 1984 (Peeters, 1993) and documented through videos (Peeters, 2008). In 2011 a case study was conducted as part of the CoRe research (Peeters & Brandt, 2011; Brandt, 2012). That case study examined the competences of childcare practitioners working with under threes in disadvantaged neighbourhoods and how these practitioners were perceived by their peers and by pedagogical counsellors as excellent workers. This research focussed especially on the acquisition of competences required to work with ethnic minorities, disadvantaged and low-income families. A focus group with four coordinators of childcare centres was set up to study professional development policies at the institutional level. Further on, biographical interviews with nine childcare workers from three different early childhood education and care (ECEC) services were organised. After one month, the researcher conducted an in depth interview with the same nine practitioners. Four core themes deriving from the biographical interviews were discussed:

1. the (changing) views about working with parents;
2. the impact of working with children and families in disadvantaged neighbourhoods;

3. learning in the initial training and in practice; and
4. the openness towards other visions and values.

In total, over 16 hours of interviews and focus groups were transcribed. The last phase of the study consisted of contextualising the data with the coordinators of the childcare services, and with the coordinator of the Pedagogical Guidance Centre, who was responsible for CPD of childcare practitioners in the city of Ghent.

The results of those different studies on the CPD system are used in this chapter, together with documents of the Pedagogical Guidance Centre of Ghent, which is responsible for the CPD initiatives.

But first, we give a short historical overview of the history of ECEC in the Flemish Community of Belgium in general and in the city of Ghent in particular.

The Flemish Community of Belgium at a glance

Belgium is a federal state. Policy area such as family services, childcare services, education, youth work and welfare are regulated at the community level. Basically, the same kind of services is offered to families in all three (Dutch, French and German speaking) communities, but different emphases or nuances exist. The three communities of Belgium all have a distinct system for ECEC. Under this split system (UNESCO, 2010), the childcare facilities for children from birth to three years old are the responsibility of the Department of Welfare, with governmental organisations being responsible for the quality of the policy: *Office de la Naissance et de l'Enfance*, *Fédération Wallonie-Bruxelles* (French-speaking part), *Kind en Gezin*, Flemish Community of Belgium (Dutch-speaking part), *Kind und Familie*, German Community of Belgium (German-speaking part). Pre-primary education (*kleuterscholen, écoles maternelles*) from two and a half years old to mandatory school age (six years) is the responsibility of the Department of Education and is integrated in the system of elementary education (two and a half until twelve years).

High enrolment

Belgium is one of the six Member States that achieved both objectives of the Barcelona Targets, with 99% of enrolment in pre-primary education and nearly 40% in childcare (European Parliament, 2013). Even in times of economic crisis, policy makers, researchers and stakeholders in Belgium have invested in increasing accessibility for vulnerable groups and in making childcare and pre-primary education affordable for all parents. In Flanders, the implementation of the new law on childcare (*Decreet Kinderopvang voor baby's en peuters*) in April 2014 aims at universal provision by 2020 and a unique quality monitoring system for all types of home-based and centre-based childcare services.

The provision of structural services for the entire population, as well as providing additional funding towards disadvantaged groups, appears to be the most effective strategy for making ECEC accessible, especially for children from immigrant background or low-income families (Leseman, 2009; Vandenbroeck & Lazzari, 2014). For the childcare sector, the Flemish government decided early 2009, to take structural and legislative measures. Ever since, all funded childcare centres are obliged to reserve 20% of their capacity for single-parent families and families living in poverty and in crisis situations. In the subsidised sector (80% of the childcare places) of the Flemish Community, the parents contribute between 5 euros[1] and 27,36 euros a day, according to their income. The private childcare centres, which receive no grants, can freely set their price. The costs of childcare (from birth to three years old and out of school care) are tax deductible: all child-care costs are 100% deductible with a maximum of 11,20 euros a day.

The pre-primary school from two and a half until six is cost-free, except for meals and extracurricular activities.

In pre-primary education, a bachelor qualification is required. The pre-primary teachers receive almost the same salary as teachers in primary and second-ary schools. Consequently, one could say that the level of qualification necessary to be a pre-primary teacher is high and the working conditions are good, compared to other European Member States. However, in the childcare sector, the level of qualification required is problematic. In several international reports (OECD, 2001, 2006; UNICEF, 2008), it was mentioned that the qualification level of staff in Belgian childcare is unacceptably low (16 years plus three). The situation in Flanders is even worse, as there are no qualification requirements in family day care and in the former independent childcare sector. In the former subsidised childcare centres (only 17% of the childcare places), pre-service training on post-secondary vocational level (one year) is mandatory. In 2008 a research on professionalism in Flemish childcare concluded that the initial training was not able to prove an added value (Peeters, 2008) and in 2010 the governmental organisation took the initiative to unite representatives of the sector and the schools. The results of this survey came to one conclusion: the training is not able to meet the needs of the field (Kind en Gezin, 2010). The new decree on childcare (2014) finally stipulates that all childcare workers should have a qualification, but this will only be imple-mented in 2024.

The next section gives a historical overview of childcare in the city of Ghent, where a coherent policy was developed to increase the level of professionalism in childcare centres, despite the low level of initial training.

Ghent takes the lead in a coherent CPD policy

In the municipality of Ghent, the low level of initial training has been supplemented successfully with CPD. More than 35 years of intensive pedagogical counselling of childcare staff resulted in innovative practices regarding outreach to families in poverty, ethnic minority families and families of children with special needs. We go back in recent history to describe the context of this successful investment in professionalisation. In the early 1970s, the city council took the initiative of start-ing a Pedagogical Guidance Centre (PGC) for municipal schools. The pedagogical quality of the education system in the 1960s and early 1970s was very poor and the Alderman wanted to improve the results of working-class children in these schools. The city council unfolded ambitious plans with the 'Pedagogical Guidance Centre' and engaged three scientific collaborators from the Ghent University holding a PhD: a pedagogue and two developmental psychologists. Since childcare was integrated in the education system, the PGC was also in charge of the childcare centres. In 1979, the PGC decided to participate in an OMEP (*Organisation Mondiale de l'Éducation Préscolaire*) study on the quality of day-care centres and out-of-school centres. The results of the OMEP research showed an extreme emphasis on medical-hygienic aspects in childcare centres, the absence of any form of participation by parents and a very child-unfriendly approach (Peeters, 1993). In autumn 1979 the Faculty of Psychology and Educational Sciences of Ghent University set up an action-research project in collaboration with the PGC. The action research project was theoretically inspired by social constructivism and by the notion of the 'teacher-as-researcher' (Stenhouse, 1975) and the Freirian notion of 'cultural action'. These frameworks were put into practice in adult education through democratic, participative and experiential training methods. Some of the guiding principles included:

1. avoiding the hierarchical dichotomy between researchers (who took the role of pedagogical counsellors) and practitioners;
2. involving practitioners in debates, reflecting on their everyday work; and
3. documenting their experiences as actors of change.

(Peeters, 2008)

In 1984, Ghent University evaluated the effects of the pedagogical counselling in the action-research projects and the researchers concluded that the collaboration between pedagogical counsellors and practitioners had had a very positive effect on increasing the level of competences in practitioners with low qualifications (secondary vocational level) (Peeters, 1993), and as a result, the PGC developed a comprehensive policy for continuous professional development (De Meyer, 2012).

The competent system in Ghent: involving every level

Over the past 35 years, the PGC gradually developed a multi-layered competent system that involves all the people working in ECEC: individual practitioners, teams, heads of centres, district-coordinators, the director of the childcare unit and the local policy makers.

A brief overview will guide the reader through the different levels of the Ghent competent system.

On the level of the individual practitioner/heads of centres:

*   a choice between courses and peer learning groups;
*   an introduction course for new practitioners and heads of centres.

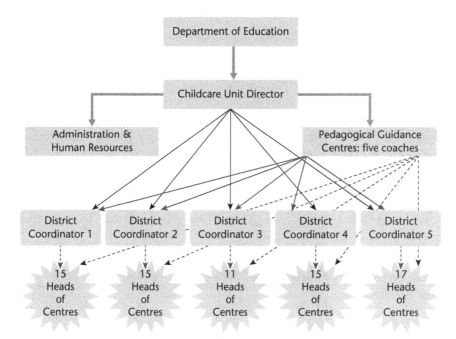

FIGURE 4.1   Organisation chart of the Childcare Unit of the Department of
Education, City of Ghent

All workers of the services are provided with a wide range of courses concerning children, parents, teams and the community. They can choose between two different models: courses for individual workers and peer groups for workers representing their institution. The childcare sector is expanding in Ghent: even in times of economic crisis new centres open and new workers are hired. In order to get informed and grow familiar with the mission, vision and organisation of ECEC in Ghent, new practitioners and new heads of centres are obliged to attend a four-day training course.

On the team / institution level:

- pedagogical study day for the whole team of the centre;
- coaching to reflect upon practice;
- coaching of changing processes;
- courses for new teams;
- introducing new pedagogical approaches.

The PGC strongly promotes the combination of a 'Pedagogical Study day' for the whole workforce of the centre with coaching in teams afterwards. This approach is an effective form of CPD in order to change the pedagogical practice and has had a clear impact on collegiality and teamwork: the practitioners are actively involved, which has proved to be effective in improving the educational practice.

On demand, a pedagogical counsellor can support a team during the process of change. Prior to the coaching, the counsellor profoundly explores the questions of the staff and formulates the goals of the coaching process. Afterwards, the counsellor makes a proposal describing the content, methods and duration of the coaching process. The actual coaching is carried out by the pedagogical counsellor or by the head of the centre.

The PGC also organises week courses for teams of new childcare centres. During this week, members of the new team develop a common pedagogical vision. This is achieved through reflections on study visits, discussions about vision and about how to put the vision into practice. Through developing this common pedagogical approach within the specific context, the team of the new childcare centre is prepared to welcome children and parents in appropriate ways. The programme of this week-long course is developed by the pedagogical counsellor of the team in cooperation with the head of the centre.

On the city level (Childcare Unit of the Department of Education/PGC)

The city level involves:

- learning communities for the pedagogical counsellors, the middle management and the practitioners: organising peer groups and intervision groups;
- organisation of a Pedagogical Conference every two years for the whole workforce of all municipal centres;
- implementing new pedagogical approaches;
- development of tools;
- meetings between pedagogical counsellors and staff of the Childcare Unit, the Department of Education and policy makers.

In the new millennium, the investment of the city in a support structure for the services was continued through the creation of the 'Dienst Kinderopvang' – the Childcare Unit, a sub-department within the Department of Education. The first director of the Childcare Unit was established in 2002 and in 2006 the director received the support of a middle management of five persons at bachelor level, each of them working as a coordinator in a specific district of the town. Each pedagogical counsellor is also connected to a district of the town and works in close cooperation with that district coordinator. The duos prepare monthly meetings for the heads of centres, taking into account a good balance between pedagogical and organisational themes. Together they involve the participants by using new coaching methods and by introducing new tools that can be useful to heads of centres or staff members in the team meetings of their institution. The roles of the duos in the meeting are specifically assigned: the pedagogical counsellor is the group facilitator and the district coordinator is the leader of the group.

A Pedagogical Conference is organised every two years for the whole work-force of the childcare sector of the city of Ghent. In this Pedagogical Conference, practitioners from different services present in workshops innovative projects to colleagues of other day-care centres. These workshops are the result of a process of change that was developed during the team meetings in the different childcare centres.

Over the last few years, the district meetings shifted to what is called in litera-ture, a learning community (Brajkovic, 2014) in which heads of centres learn from each other and develop a common vision on pedagogical, social and organisational matters.

The PGC also plays an important role in implementing new pedagogical approaches towards all day-care centres. Services which want to experiment with innovative approaches, receive coaching by a pedagogical counsellor over a period of four years, as was the case in the North Italian documentation approach (Malavasi & Zoccatelli, 2013) and the Wanda method (Sharmahd, et al., 2015), a coaching method that is based on an appreciative inquiry (Cooperrider & Whitney, 2001) and on critically analysing the pedagogical practice (Barbier, 2006). In support for the introduction of this new approach, the coach meets the practitioners every week, facilitates team meetings, and organises pedagogical conferences, study vis-its and supervision for directors of centres. Once the innovative approach is fully tested, it will be disseminated to other centres and then the coaching of the team becomes less intensive.

Peer groups with a focus on exchanging interesting practices among different childcare centres, are highly appreciated by practitioners and are powerful tools in changing pedagogical practices. Over the years, the peer groups evolved into supervision groups. Pedagogical counsellors support different supervision groups: e.g. for heads of centres sharing a common pedagogical approach, for mentors of trainees or for practitioners focussing on the active participation of young children. The counsellors support the teams by creating a safe atmosphere where reflection on practice leads to new knowledge and innovative practices.

Therefore, a resource centre was set up within the PGC. The coaches devel-oped a large number of instruments: boxes with didactical materials and games to use in coaching sessions, ICT applications and booklets for the children in the out-of-school centres. Over the years practitioners and heads of centres were getting more involved in the development of these tools. The Childcare Unit also pub-lished booklets and videos for parents about different topics and more specifically, for parents from poor and minority backgrounds.

Monthly meetings are organised with the whole staff of the Department of Education and the policy makers of the city and with the pedagogical coun-sellors. Policy priorities and pedagogical targets are discussed, evaluated and adjusted. CPD initiatives for all the childcare centres are developed based on common themes and the role of each part of the organisation in the process of change is fixed.

On the level of the Flemish Community

Participation of the Childcare Service in advisory groups of governmental organisations

The counsellors and district coordinators are members of many advisory groups: on the social function of childcare; on inclusive childcare; on competences profiles of the childcare worker; on new legislation on childcare; and on the new quality framework for children from birth to three years old; and many others.

International networks and European innovation projects

Since the beginning of the 1990s, the PGC has been active in many international networks. In workshops and conferences outside Flanders, counsellors have shared the good practice of Ghent. Ghent receives visitors from all over the world and in 2013 it hosted the first Transatlantic Forum on Inclusive Early Years (Peeters & Vandekerckhove, 2015). The city was involved in four different transnational European Social Fund projects, in the DECET network on diversity in ECEC (www.decet.org) and also in the Reyn Network for Roma children from the ISSA Network (www.issa.nl/content/reyn). This active participation in international networks is of major importance. It has inspired the pedagogical coaches in their work with the teams and with practitioners and directors, and has led to many innovations in childcare centres in Ghent. The recognition of the municipal approach in international reports (OECD, 2001, 2006; UNESCO, 2010; Urban et al., 2011) valorises the efforts of practitioners, head of centres and policy makers in Ghent and also stimulates the local policy makers to continue to invest in the development of a competent system in the ECEC field.

Critical factors that make pedagogical coaching and professional learning work

From the evaluations of 35 years of experience with coaching and CPD in general, some critical factors that make professional learning effective can be identified.

First, during the CPD and especially the coaching sessions, the practitioners should be able to express themselves freely in an open dialogue, and the culture of the team must be valorised. Therefore the counsellors need to have an appreciative approach and the coaches need to have a strong confidence in the capabilities and the engagement of the practitioners.

Second, the policy of the PGC states that effective CPD should fit the mission and vision of the local organisation, underpinned by a framework of principles and values. This quality framework must be sufficiently broad and open, so that practitioners and teams are challenged to discover, to discuss and to engage themselves in developing a common vision and practice, a common culture based on common values.

The current quality framework of the Childcare Unit in Ghent is the result of a process of two years of reflecting and discussing with a delegation of heads of centres and practitioners. The vision, principles and values are discussed and put into practice in every team. The creation of a common vision, based on common values, that is embraced by all actors, is an ongoing process that involves every actor.

A third critical factor for effective CPD is the ownership of the change. In Latin countries, it is a tradition that pedagogical counselling takes place in a non-hierarchical position. In Northern Italy (Reggio, Pistoia, Florence) – where the famous 'pedagogistas' are in charge of the pedagogical counselling – there are no head of centres in the centres (Musatti & Mayer, 2003; Terzi, 2006). Also in France, the pedagogical coaches, involved in the analyses of practice (*analyse des pratiques*) do not have a hierarchical position towards the practitioners they are coaching (Fablet, 2004; Favre, 2004; see elsewhere in this book). Although these practices are based upon a long tradition in pedagogical coaching in ECEC, it does not mean that heads of centres cannot carry out coaching. In the world of Human Resource Management, coaching and leadership are often linked, and it is not uncommon that managers take up a coaching role within their hierarchical position (Blanchard, 2007; Van Den Broeck & Venter, 2011).

The policy of the city of Ghent towards the role of the head of centres changed since they began pedagogical counselling in 1979. In the beginning the coach was always someone external, who could not have a hierarchical position towards the practitioners. Some of the heads of centres and staff members collaborated intensively with the counsellors to increase the pedagogical quality of their childcare centre. Others experienced them rather as a threat to their hierarchal position as head of centres. In those centres the innovation stopped when the support of the pedagogical counsellor on the project ended. Therefore the PGC valorised the role of the director in the process of change. He or she had to take up the leadership of the process of change. As a consequence, the differences between the role of the head of centre and pedagogical counsellor have to be clearly defined. Heads of centres are leaders of ECEC centres: they co-ordinate the practical daily activities of the centre and they execute organisational and administrative tasks. Heads of centres organise team meetings and evaluate the practitioners. In cooperation with the practitioners they implement the pedagogical vision and the quality framework in practice.

Democratic leadership helps the heads of centres reduce the tension that can rise between the role of counsellor and evaluator, it creates a safe atmosphere of open communication. External counsellors may coach heads of centres and/or support the team, but only on demand and in close cooperation with the heads of centres or the internal coach. Pedagogical counsellors play a specific role in supporting and coaching heads of centres and teams in developing their pedagogical vision and constructing new pedagogical practice. As a coach or facilitator they create a culture of mutual learning. Pedagogical counsellors combine a broad knowledge on ECEC and group processes and dynamics, with the competence to use different models of coaching (Wanda, documentation…) that stimulate reflective thinking.

The pedagogical counsellors work together with other coaches in the PGC. They attend intervision, go to conferences, are active in international networks and attend training. As a result, they develop a broad view on ECEC, which enables them to construct new pedagogical knowledge. External coaches are not only working on the team level but also on the level of the Childcare Unit.

How do practitioners learn in a competent system?

In the last part of this chapter we describe the results of a case study. In this part of the CoRe study, the views of nine practitioners were analysed. This study aimed at 'how, what and where' of learning opportunities during the full career of practitioners. The study revealed important information about the opportunities and experiences of practitioners with the competent system of the city of Ghent (Peeters & Brandt, 2011; Brandt, 2012). Furthermore, this study illustrates the specific competences they developed through the very different CPD initiatives. Recently, the results of this case study were combined with the results of a survey among 50 practitioners working in contexts of diversity and poverty in ten countries (DECET & ISSA, 2011). The researchers concluded that four competences are fundamental when working with children and families:

1. openness towards parents;
2. engagement to work towards social change;
3. the ability to reflect critically; and
4. the ability to create new practices and knowledge.

(Peeters & Sharmahd, 2014)

We used these four competences to categorise the results of the present case study.

(1) Openness towards parents: the dialogue with parents as a source of professionalisation

Practitioners become sensitive and receptive to what really matters for parents in the education of their child. From a viewpoint of open communication and negotiation with parents, they construct a common approach.
Practitioners put it this way:

> Parents are the first educators of their children; therefore they must hear their voice on what is done in the childcare centre. We cannot meet all the wishes of the parents but we examine together how far we can go.

> Once you realise that by listening to the parents the relationship with the child gets better, then it is obvious that you learn from communicating with parents. The limits of how far one can go in following the parents' opinions are discussed in the team itself. If something is difficult for us, we discuss it with the pedagogical counsellor

If parents see that their child is happy when leaving in the evening, then the parents are satisfied and then I am also going home with a happy feeling.

(2) An engagement towards social change: the development of a common culture of openness, based on the conviction that every professional can make the difference

For the practitioners, the creation of a common culture in the Childcare Service and the childcare institutions is a crucial factor for effective professional learning. This culture is underpinned by a clear pedagogical vision and by a set of values on working with parents, children and the neighbourhood.

This common culture functions as an inspirational framework for the recruitment of new workforce, for training, supervision groups, pedagogical conferences and team meetings. Pedagogical counsellors and directors support teams to reflect and evaluate this vision, to translate it into the practice of their particular context.

The most important value of this common culture is the conviction that every professional can make a difference for a child, for parents and for colleagues. The practitioners state that when they become actors of change in the life of children and adults, this pertains to a greater motivation in professional development.

A practitioner talks about the openness to parents, it means to her to 'really *have lived in a group*'. When she was asked what she meant, she answered:

To be myself, and at the same time to make the difference for the others, to accept in a relation the other as being different.

Working in ECEC centres involves teamwork. In teams with a common culture of openness and open dialogue, practitioners are stimulated to experiment, colleagues can reflect on and discuss openly on each other's pedagogical interventions. This occurs in a safe atmosphere, which is a source for learning for the new colleagues.

A new member of a team puts it this way:

That feeling of being accepted increases your self-confidence and this helped me to communicate better with the parents and this again reinforced my self-confidence.

Democratic leadership of directors, appreciative and participative approaches of counsellors, appreciative approaches can help to create a safe atmosphere to speak openly and freely, to discuss, to disagree.

(3) The ability to reflect critically

The interviewees stated that crucial aspects of the job – like working with parents, communicating and negotiating and working in a context of diversity – is not learned at school but is the result of pedagogical guidance. They prefer active forms of learning: not by theory but by reflection on practice.

> You learn by stealing from the experiences of colleagues.

Practitioners declare they like to learn in an informal way through practice, by sharing knowledge and reflecting together with colleagues. Directors have an important role to support this process of reflecting in a team:

> Because childcare practitioners work permanently in a team, they must be able to rely on each other, to support each other and this attitude of team work determines the learning style that the practitioners prefer.

An experienced practitioner concludes:

> I was lucky, at the time when I started to work in the childcare of the city of Ghent, my director sent me to a colleague group on diversity and in this group I visited different childcare centres in Brussels and in other places. So I have seen a lot of good practices and through the discussions we had during study visits, I learned a lot by the work-experience itself.

(4) The ability to create new practices and knowledge

The different CPD initiatives challenge practitioners to increase their professionalism and to develop new relations with parents, children, colleagues and the neighbourhood and this enables them to create new pedagogical practices and knowledge.

> Problems are always talked through with parents; we are looking together for solutions, because in most cases there are no clear cut solutions.

Conclusions

The CoRe case study on the municipal childcare in Ghent (Peeters & Brandt, 2011) concluded that practitioners learn best when they operate in a competent system. This is characterised by a coherent multi-layered and diversified policy towards CPD, during a sustained period of time, supported by specialised pedagogical counsellors. An important critical success factor is the ownership of the change, which must be shared within the childcare centres.

The competent system of the city of Ghent is furthermore characterised by a common culture on different levels of the system. This culture is underpinned by a common vision, by ethical values towards children, parents, colleagues and the neighbourhood. It strives for social change on all levels of the competent system. The competent system must give opportunities on different levels for open communication and negotiation with all actors, in order to create new practice and knowledge. On the level of the teams two critical factors for success are essential: a vision on learning, starting from practice with a focus on sharing experiences with colleagues in and between the centres, and a constant team reflection on the daily practice.

Taking into account the conclusions of the Eurofound systematic review on CPD (2015, see the Introduction to this book), we can conclude that the city of Ghent is on the right track. Long-term pedagogical support by specialised counsellors, which starts from a focus on reflection on practice, can be an effective way to critically explore the link between theory and practice in the staff's everyday work and is an effective way to improve the pedagogical practice. From the Eurofound study, we also learn that a CPD approach like the one developed in Ghent, built upon a common vision that is based on scientific evidence and also adapted to the local needs, is quite effective. From the CoRe study (Urban et al., 2011) we learned that a competent system requires policies that effectively address the entire ECEC system and that an investment in leadership capacity at all layers of the system, is of key importance. Based on the recommendations and results of both European studies, we conclude that the Ghent approach, which is characterised by a coherent and multi-layered system of CPD, is in line with both studies and could be described as effective.

Note

1 This can be reduced to 1,56 euros for parents in financial or medical need.

References

Barbier, J.-M. (2006). Problématique identitaire et engagement des sujets dans les activités. In J.-M. Barbier, E. Bourgeois, G. De Villiers & M. Kaddouri (eds.), *Constructions identitaires et mobilisation des sujets en formation* (pp. 15–64). Paris: L'Harmattan.

Blanchard, K. (2007). *Leading at a higher level: Blanchard on leadership and creating high performing organisation.* Upper Saddle River, NJ: Pearson Education.

Brajkovic, S. (2014). *Professional learning communities.* Leiden: ISSA.

Brandt, S.T. (2012). Perspectieven op leren en groei: een casestudie over competenties van kindbegeleiders in 3 goede praktijken in de Gentse kinderopvang. Universiteit Gent: unpublished dissertation.

Cooperrider, D.L. & Whitney, D. (2001). A positive revolution in change. In D.L. Cooperrider, P. Sorenson, D. Whitney & T. Yeager (eds.), *Appreciative inquiry: an emerging direction for organisation development* (pp. 9–29). Champaign, IL: Stipes.

DECET & ISSA (2011). *Diversity and social inclusion: exploring competences for professional practice in ECEC.* Brussels & Budapest: Author. Retrieved, November 2013, from http://www.decet.org/fileadmin/decet-media/publications/Diversity-and-Social Inclusion.pdf.

De Meyer, A. (2012). The ECEC system in Ghent. Ghent: unpublished dissertation for study visit of US foundations.

European Parliament DG Internal policies (2013). *Barcelona targets revisited.* Brussels: European Parliament.

Eurofound (2015). *Early childhood care: working conditions, training and quality – a systematic review*. Dublin: Eurofound.

Fablet, D. (ed.) (2004). *Professionnel(le)s de la petite enfance et analyse de pratiques*. Paris: L'Harmattan.

Favre, D. (2004). Quelques réflexions de formateur sur l'analyse des pratiques professionnelles en secteur petite enfance. In D. Fablet (ed.), *Professionnel(le)s de la petite enfance et analyse de pratiques* (pp. 17–38). Paris: L'Harmattan.

Kind en Gezin (2010). Rapport over 7ᵉ jaar BSO Kinderzorg. Brussels: unpublished report.

Leseman, P.P.M. (2009). The impact of high quality education and care on the development of young children: review of the literature. In Eurydice and EACEA, *Early childhood education and care in Europe: tackling social and cultural inequalities* (pp. 17–49). Brussels: EACEA.

Malavasi, L. & Zoccatelli, B. (2013). *Documenteren voor jonge kinderen*. Amsterdam: SWP.

Musatti, T. & Mayer, S. (2003). *Il coordinamento dei servizi educativi per l'infanzia: una funzione emergente in Italia e in Europa*. Bergamo: Edizioni Junior.

OECD (2001). *Starting strong I: early childhood education and care*. Paris: OECD.

OECD (2006). *Starting strong II: early childhood education and care*. Paris: OECD.

Peeters, J. (1993). Quality improvements in the day care centres with the support of the Bernard van Leer Foundation. In J. Peeters & M. Vandenbroeck (eds.), *Working towards better childcare: report about 13 years of research and training* (pp. 39–79). Ghent: RUG, VBJK.

Peeters, J. (2008). *De warme professional begeleid(st)ers kinderopvang construeren professionaliteit*. Ghent: Academia Press.

Peeters, J. & Vandenbroeck, M. (2010). *Caring and learning together: a case study of Ghent – the Flemish community of Belgium. Early Childhood and Family Policy Series*. Vol. 20. Paris: UNESCO.

Peeters, J. & Brandt, S. (2011). *Report on the case study Ghent*. Ghent: VBJK.

Peeters, J. & Vandenbroeck, M. (2012). Childcare practitioners and the process of professionalisation. In L. Miller, R. Dury & C. Cable (eds.), *Extending professional practice in the early years* (pp. 99–112). Los Angeles, London, New Delhi, Singapore, Washington DC: Sage and Open University.

Peeters, J. & Sharmahd, N. (2014). Professional Development for ECEC practitioners with responsibilities for children at risk: which competences and in-service training are needed. *European Early Childhood Education Research Journal, 22* (3), 412–424.

Peeters, J. & Vandekerckhove, A. (2015). A meeting place for policy makers and researchers: a transatlantic forum for inclusive early years. *International Journal for Early Years Education*, 23(3), 329–337.

Stenhouse, L. (1975). *An introduction to curriculum research and development*. London: Heinemann.

Sharmahd N., Van Laere K., De Schepper, B. & Vastmans, S. (2015). *Using the Wanda method in professional learning communities: the road to quality – strengthening professionalism in early childhood education and care systems by using Issa's quality resource pack*. Ghent: VBJK Arteveldehogeschool.

Terzi, N. (ed.) (2006). *Prospettive di qualità al nido: il ruolo del coordinatore educativo*. Bergamo: Edizioni Junior.

UNESCO (2010). *Caring and learning together: a cross-national study of integration of ECEC within education*. Paris: UNESCO.

UNICEF Innocenti Research Centre (2008). *Report card 8: the childcare transition*. Florence: UNICEF.

Urban, M., Vandenbroeck, M., Peeters, J., Lazzari, A. & Van Laere, K. (2011). *CoRe final report*. Brussels: European Commission.

Van Den Broeck, H. & Venter, D. (2011). *Beyonders, transcending, average, leadership*. Leuven: Lannoo Campus Blanchard.

Vandenbroeck, M., Boudry, C., De Brabandere, K. & Vens, N. (2010). *L'inclusion des enfants ayant des besoins spécifiques*. Ghent: VBJK.

Vandenbroeck, M, & Lazzari, A. (2014). Accessibility of early childhood education and care: a state of affairs. *European Early Childhood Education Research Journal, 22*(3): 327–335.

5

EARLY CHILDHOOD EDUCATION AND CARE STAFF WITH DIFFERENT QUALIFICATIONS IN PROFESSIONAL DEVELOPMENT PROCESSES

Tatjana Vonta

Introduction: early childhood education and care in Slovenia

Slovenia has established an integrated approach to early childhood education and care (ECEC) for children from one to six years of age, combining education, play and care in preschool institutions. Enrolment in a preschool institution is not compulsory. Preschools are established and financed by municipalities and parent contributions (from 0 to 80 percent, depending on their income), from the national budget (for specific purposes like transport of preschool children) and from donations and other sources. Municipalities can establish three different types of preschool institutions:

- free-standing preschool institutions (with more than ten groups of children);
- a preschool unit located in a primary school, or
- a unit of a preschool institution (with few classrooms, located in buildings away from the main preschool institution).

Preschools can offer various programmes of different organisation and duration. The whole day programme lasts between six and nine hours, and a half-day programme lasts from four to six hours and includes education, care and food. In remote and demographically distant areas preschools can offer shorter programmes that last from 240 to 600 hours per year for children from three years until primary school enrolment. Finally, they also can offer family care programmes that take place at the home of the preschool teacher or teacher assistant. In these cases, professional staff are employed at the preschool institution.

Public preschools and private preschools with a concession (authorised to be engaged in public service programmes) implement the national Preschool Curriculum. It represents goals, principles and basic knowledge about the development of the child and about learning in the preschool age, global goals and the derived goals for six defined areas of learning (physical exercise, language, art, society, nature study and mathematics). Each area of learning includes separate goals and examples of activities for children aged from one to three years and for children from three to six years, as well as for the role of the professional staff in the classroom (for example: how to observe children, how to support interactions and creativity, how to build a sense of inclusiveness and cooperation, etc.). The curriculum sees the child as an active participant in the process, who gains new skills and knowledge by exploring, testing and choosing by himself/herself. The educational process, interactions and experiences from which the child learns are the focus of the curriculum (Kurikulum za vrtce, 1999).

Preschool institutions are organised into first (one to three years) and second age groups (three to six years). The kind and the number of groups and the number of children per group are regulated by legally determined norms and standards. The group size may be increased by two children per classroom if there are too many children on the waiting list. The number of children per group varies according to the children's ages, from 12 children in the first age group to 22 for the second.

A preschool teacher and a preschool teacher's assistant make up the classroom staff. In a whole day programme, they work simultaneously in the classroom for at least four to six hours depending on the age group. In a half-day programme, they work simultaneously in the classroom for two to three hours depending on the age group. A preschool teacher should work directly with children for 30 hours per week and a teacher's assistant for 35 hours per week. Preschool teachers should hold an advanced two-year studies qualification (ISCED level 5, abolished in 1992), a higher education degree (ISCED level 6) in preschool education (in place since 1995) or a university degree (ISCED level 7) in preschool education or some other field (pedagogy, art, humanities, sociology) with a specialisation in preschool education. Preschool teachers can also teach children in the first grade of compulsory school together with a primary school teacher. The required qualification for a preschool teacher's assistant is an upper secondary vocational qualification in preschool education (ISCED level 4) or general upper secondary school and pass for a vocational course on working with preschool children (Zakon o vrtcih, 1996). Additionally, in environments with populations of Romani children, a Roma assistant should be involved in preschools and primary schools (Strategija izobraževanja Romov v Republiki Sloveniji, 2004). Thus, in reality preschool classroom staff can have very different qualifications.

According to the Collective Agreement for the Education Sector in the Republic of Slovenia (Kolektivna pogodba, 1994), professional staff have the right to at least 5 days of continuous professional training per year or 15 days every three years. Through further continuous professional development (CPD), professional staff can gain additional points (if training is accredited), which are taken into account for advancement opportunities. Preschool teachers can be promoted to mentor, adviser and councillor. In order to achieve those titles, they collect points

defined by the Collective Agreement for the Education Sector (mostly for participation in training, projects, professional conferences, publishing articles, organising
events with children, etc.). Unfortunately, the gained titles are permanent and
to some extent influence only an increase of income but have no influence on
working obligations. The fact that professional titles are permanent and unchange-
able does not encourage CPD and needs to be changed. Furthermore, there is no
promotional system for teachers' assistants (Pravilnik o napredovanju zaposelnih v
vzgoji in izobraževanju, 2002). The salary of a preschool teacher is much higher
than the salary of a teacher's assistant.

By law (Zakon o organizaciji in financiranju vzgoje in izobraževanja, 1994),
the head teacher is responsible for promoting the professional development of
staff, observing their practice, monitoring and consulting them and ensuring and
monitoring quality through self-evaluation. Within the yearly work plan, the head
teacher is obliged to plan training for professional staff and to enable them to participate. In cases where a preschool unit is operating at a primary school, the primary
school head teacher is also responsible for quality improvement and professional
development of preschool staff, but they also have a vice-head teacher or head of
the preschool unit who is responsible for the preschool unit and usually works part
time directly with children.

Further education and training for staff is provided with support in accordance
with the national Regulation (Pravilnik o nadaljnjem izobraževanju in spopolnjevanju, 2004) in order to support quality and efficiency of professional staff. The
Ministry of Education financially supports various courses like further training,
professional training, thematic conferences, study groups, networks and computer
literacy courses. Some of those courses are free of charge and some have to be
paid for, in most cases by preschools and very seldom by the participants. Courses
providers include higher education institutions, the National Education Institute,
the Educational Research Institute, the School for Headmasters and non-profit and
private organisations.

The purpose of the study

For almost 20 years, the Developmental Research Centre for Pedagogical Initiatives
at the Educational Research Institute in Ljubljana has provided various activities
for preschools and their staff in order to support quality improvement, CPD and
sharing experiences of good practices. We set up the Step by Step Network, which
includes more than 1,000 professionals from around forty preschools. Members can
choose to participate in training, workshops, professional meetings, conferences,
visits, observations with reflections, consulting activities, cooperation among
members, action research and other research projects, etc. In all those activities, we
strive to involve head teachers, teachers and teachers' assistants. The framework for
quality improvement activities is based on International Step by Step Association
quality principles (ISSA, 2010) and ISSA's Quality Resource Pack, continuous
needs assessments among network members and research work. The centre focuses

on supporting processes for quality improvement and professional development as well as workplace learning.

Through regular monitoring and observation of practice in network members' classrooms, we recognised that there are big differences in quality improvement processes and the level of changes they implement. For assessment in the classroom, we use ISSA's quality assessment instrument. In this case study, we analysed critical factors in the professional development processes of staff and in the quality improvement processes of early childhood education and care at the level of preschool institutions. In this framework, we placed special attention on diversity of the qualifications of staff who work together in the same classroom in very different organisational contexts, conditions and support systems.

We collected data in three preschools and one primary school in various parts of Slovenia: in two large towns, one smaller town and one smaller settlement. Two of the three preschools are freestanding preschool institutions, while one preschool unit is located in a primary school. In the freestanding preschools, we collected data in one classroom from the first age group and in one classroom from the second age group. In the preschool unit at a primary school, we collected data in one classroom with combined age groups. All preschools and the primary school have been involved in our network for more than ten years. The head teachers of all four institutions have changed during those years, but the new head teachers from independent preschools have involved themselves in many activities at the network level, while the new primary school head teachers were not actively involved in those activities.

To gain better insight into various contexts, we collected general information and opinions of staff and head teachers on the policy of their institution in regard to quality assurance and concern for professional development. Our multiple sources database consists of data collected through guided interviews with professional staff (13 interviews), head teachers (4 interviews) and randomly selected children from each of the groups monitored (29 interviews), as well as through anonymous questionnaires for parents (in total, 30 of them were distributed, but only 17 parents sent the questionnaires back) and through direct observation within groups (six observations).

In order to gain data, we prepared protocols for guided interviews, questionnaires for parents and observation forms for observations in the classroom. Four experienced researchers with highly reliable observation and evaluation skills performed data collection and observations.

Conditions for professional development in different settings

Preschool A

Setting A is the largest preschool in a larger city and is organised into seven preschool units at different locations. At the time when we conducted the study, there were 36 classrooms, 14 of them for the first age group and 22 for the second age group, and 80 professional staff employed. The working hours are from 5:30 am to 4:30 pm. The preschool offers only a whole-day programme, because few parents are interested in a short programme.

The head teacher told us that all professional staff are included in self-evaluation training and active learning strategies, and nearly half of them implement Step by Step approaches in realising the National Curriculum. The preschool is also involved in many different innovation projects. They stimulate daily reflection of work in staff tandems, prepare and organise workshops at the preschool level, introduce observation and reflection of their own or other teachers' practice through video clips, stimulate critical reflection according to ISSA's quality principles and the guidelines of the Step by Step Network and carry out evaluations of projects and priority assignments every six months. For the head teacher, those activities have an important influence on the quality of professional practice. Staff can choose by themselves which training they wish to attend and in which projects they wish to participate. She also stressed that staff have enough time for daily reflection, which takes place when the children are taking a rest, while the weekly tandem meeting for planning and reflection takes place outside of the classroom, usually during rest time. During tandem meetings, someone else from the preschool's professional staff takes over their classroom. The tandem meetings, and the schedule of replacements during the meetings, are scheduled individually and last for approximately one hour. The conditions for these kinds of meetings are not optimal, as there is insufficient space and a lack of computers.

Answers to the research question about staff's professional development were also collected by the staff in a classroom of the first age group. The classroom staff included a preschool teacher with 35 years of working experience and an ISCED level 5 education, and a teacher's assistant with an ISCED level 4 education and one year of working experience. She was also finishing a higher educational programme in the field of preschool education. The teacher and the assistant had been working together for one year. Both mentioned the same forms of professional development (reading literature, observation of their own practice with the help of video-tape-analysis, participating in seminars, cooperating in team meetings). They were free to decide which seminars or training to attend, although the management also had a say in it. Both believed they got enough professional training, but the preschool teacher mentioned that there are not enough seminars for the first age group. Sometimes, they combined workshops and training. They had one hour per week for common planning and reflection during working hours. Critical reflection of their own practice was also provided on a daily basis while the children were resting.

In the classroom of the second age group, there was a preschool teacher with 21 years of working experience and an assistant with three years of working experience. Both professionals are now working together for the second year and both have only an upper secondary education (ISCED level 4). They told us that they attend various seminars and workshops, exchange information with other professionals in the preschool, use and study textbooks, observe the practices of others and discuss their observations among themselves. The preschool teacher added that she also consults an education counsellor. They told us that some of their continuous professional training is always selected by the management and is compulsory, while some they choose themselves. They believed that they received enough training, and the preschool teacher stressed that sometimes the need arises to repeat the same training. In most cases, both of them could join the same professional development meetings, workshops or training, especially when they were conducted for staff involved in Step by Step Network activities or the entire professional staff at the preschool.

Daily reflection took place during the rest time for the children for 15-20 minutes. The preschool teacher pointed out that on the basis of critical review of their own practice, they build their future planning, evaluate the realisation of set goals and processes, plan new goals and teaching and learning strategies and understand their own practice and professional roles. The teacher's assistant explained that they (she and the preschool teacher she was working with) can see if they achieved their goals, in what scope a particular activity was successful, what the children have learned and how they can further improve their teaching. They wrote down their reflections. Once per week they had time for a meeting. The preschool teacher added that she wrote down a monthly evaluation and then discussed it with her assistant. They believed they had enough time for a regular evaluation of their practice, but the preschool teacher wrote a detailed reflection and evaluation at home.

Preschool B

The preschool is located in a smaller town in five different preschool units. At the time we provided the study, there were 26 classrooms, 11 for first age group and 15 for the second age group, and fifty-nine professional staff.

The preschool's working hours are from 5:30 am to 4:15 pm, although most children go home around 3 pm. In the morning (before 7:30 am) and in the afternoon (after 3 pm), children join one or two combined groups. Preschool teachers and assistants are present at the preschool for seven and a half hours per day and have one hour for planning.

The head teacher pointed out that professional staff evaluate their work daily based on their daily reflection and planning; some of them create a professional portfolio based on ISSA's principles of quality pedagogy. She uses required in-class observations to monitor the practice and professional development of her staff, while they perform in-class observations for other colleagues. They prepare self-evaluation reports and have prepared a "plan of improvement" at the level of each classroom, working group and the whole preschool. The plan defines goals, strategies and activities as well as determining deadlines for implementation and measures for monitoring of goal-achievements. They systematically observe the achieving of set goals and determine to what extent they realise the goals. They also take part in various projects and professional training. She believes that staff don't have enough time for shared planning but have enough opportunities for critical reflection, especially at meetings for planning, team meetings, pedagogical conferences and collegial in-classroom observations and reflections. She stressed that critical evaluation and reflection improve the quality of work.

We provided interviews with staff in one classroom from the first age group. The preschool teacher had 33 years of working experience and the teacher's assistant had 27 years of working experience. They had been working together for three years. Both of them had an upper secondary education (ISCED level 4) degree. They promoted their professional development by participating in team meetings, working group meetings for the particular age groups of children and seminars. The preschool teacher also practised self-evaluation, which helped her to plan for the next school year, while the teacher's assistant pointed out the importance of in-classroom observations for professional development. The teacher's assistant felt that it was up to them to choose the seminars and training that they would like to attend. However, the preschool teacher gave a more detailed description and explained that they could choose from the seminars that the head teacher has offered. They both felt that they cared enough for their professional development and sometimes even joined a seminar together.

They did not have a specially scheduled time for common planning, and they usually discussed it during the break or during the children's rest period. The preschool teacher had one hour per day for daily planning, however her assistant had to stay in class during that time. They discussed daily anything they had done wrong and what might have caused this. When we asked them why they did this, the preschool teacher replied that it is necessary if you wish to improve your own practice and to avoid making the same mistake again. The teacher's assistant explained that this is important if you wish to improve your practice and plan it.

Within the classroom of the second age group, we interviewed a preschool teacher with 21 years of working experience and an assistant with 23 years of working experience. Both had an ISCED level 4 education. According to their answers, they took care of professional development by attending staff working groups, pedagogic conferences at the level of the school, team meetings and various seminars, and both maintained a professional portfolio into which they inserted examples of their good practice with reflections. In most cases, they could decide for themselves which training to attend. The preschool teacher added that she selects in-service training based on analysis of the previous school year. Both of them believed that there is never enough and there is never too much training. The preschool teacher said that there are many different types of training available, and that professionals should make an effort regarding their own professional development. At some educational training, both of them were present, and when this was not the case, they passed information on to each other; they also planned together the innovations that they would implement into practice and discussed their effects.

They made joint plans on what they would do the following week (based on observation of the children) during the time when the children are resting. The preschool teacher said that through the situations that occur in the classroom they find out whether they have managed to implement their goals and whether they should try to achieve them in some other manner. The preschool teacher's assistant focused on the reflection that they conclude with the children once or twice per week. She said that they talk about what the children liked and disliked. Her opinion is that this is also important and that they should write down the children's statements. The preschool teacher said that she did not have enough time for regular evaluation, while the teacher's assistant said that she has enough time to do it at home but not while at work.

Preschool C

The preschool is a unit of a primary school in a smaller settlement and has 95 enrolled children. The children enrolled in this preschool include a number of Roma children from the neighbouring settlements and villages. They have a head teacher for the whole school (preschool and primary school) as well as a head of the preschool unit, but the head teacher is in charge of overall quality assurance and improvement. The head of the preschool unit additionally works directly with the children in the classroom for 20 hours per week.

A Roma teaching assistant helps Roma children with inclusion into the preschool and primary school, supports them to overcome language difficulties and includes Roma culture and language into the curriculum. She cooperates with Roma parents, especially if they have poor or no knowledge of the Slovenian language, and takes part in various activities organised in the Roma settlement. The Roma teaching assistant was present in the classroom for four hours two days per week; on other days she was involved in similar activities in the primary classes. At the time when our study took place, the Slovenian Roma Association employed her at this school within the framework of European Social Found project, in which they offered Roma teaching assistants training in psychology, didactics, pedagogy, standard Slovenian language, ICT, inclusion of children with special needs, etc., in order to introduce them into the school system. The working time of the Roma teaching assistant is from 7 am until 3 pm every day. During school holidays, she takes part in training for Roma teaching assistants.

The head teacher emphasised that she regularly provides classroom observations, which help her determine the necessary fields of improvement. In this school year, she noticed that they would have to focus especially on the use of standard language. Although the dialect is rather nice, the professional staff will have to learn to use the standard language at work. This is of great importance because they are introducing children into the world of books, literary texts and drama plays. She regularly took part in the preschool's monthly team meetings, where all staff plan the next month's common themes and events. She strove for the greatest possible participation of staff in changing the organisation of work or educational processes, although added that not everything can be solved democratically. In such cases, she always consulted staff and was prepared to give further explanations. She found that it was very important for them to cooperate successfully in tandem, even if they are not one hundred percent compatible on a personal level, which still represented a problem in some cases. Those competences should be better developed by the staff. She was aware that self-evaluation and critical reflection are crucial, but she had to note that this is a weakness of their preschool staff. She tried to give her staff the best conditions for constructive debates, which will improve in the new building as now the professional staff's area is at the end of the hallway.

We collected information about professional development activities in a combined classroom where 14 children from one to five years old participated; four of them were Roma children. The preschool teacher had a higher education degree (ISCED level 6) and 14 years of working experience, while the teacher's assistant had an upper secondary school education (ISCED level 4) and two years of working experience. The Roma teaching assistant was a dental assistant by profession (ISCED level 4), but she had been working in the field of education for seven years. They had all been working together for two years. The preschool teacher and the teacher's assistant worked for seven and a half hours daily and spent an additional half an hour on other activities like team planning and preparations for teacher-parent conferences, etc.

The preschool teacher stressed that she cares for her professional development mainly through literature and seminars but did not receive enough practical advice regarding work in the classroom. She liked training that enables direct use in practice. The teacher's assistant had a strong wish to join any kind of training. The professional education of the Roma teaching assistant took place within the scope of the project provided by the Slovenian Roma Association. The preschool teacher and assistant did not take part in CPD together, because it is difficult to get a replacement for both of them at the same time. Both would like to have more training. The Roma teaching assistant thought that there was enough continuous professional development.

The Roma teaching assistant did not take part in the daily reflection. She pointed out the fact that there is no formal education for a Roma teaching assistant and that only experience can help them with their work. However, she believed that team planning, in which she did not take part, does not require any additional knowledge. The Roma teaching assistant took part in team meetings for the entire preschool staff, where mostly general issues were discussed. She bravely confessed that she had to ask her colleagues to tell her if she is doing something wrong and what she is doing wrong. She confessed that she learnt a lot from her colleagues and that she can still learn much from her own mistakes. The preschool teacher revealed that she does not have enough time for continuous evaluation of her own practice. After being asked why they were doing this, she answered because they were told to. However, she was convinced that it has a positive effect on the pedagogic process.

First grade of primary school

The primary school, chosen for data comparison, is located in the city centre of a big city and has approximately 300 children from first to ninth grade of compulsory primary education. Children come to the first grade from different parts of the city; almost all of them attended preschool before enrolling in primary school. They regularly employed, in addition to primary school teachers, preschool teachers for each first grade classroom. Like the primary school teachers, the preschool teachers have the same weekly pedagogic responsibility of 22 working hours. The allocation of the preschool teachers' working hours depends on certain conditions in the primary school and on the share of the above standard burden that the local community is prepared to cover. The burden is rather high in this city, which is why in our case preschool and primary school teachers spend two hours together in the classroom. The primary school teachers start class at 8:15 am. The preschool teachers join in around 10 am, and they stay together until noon, when the primary school teacher leaves. The preschool teacher stays with the children in the extended school care classroom until 2:30 pm. After 2:30 pm, children from the extended school care classrooms are placed in combined classes. Since the salary of public officials depends on the level of completed education, the preschool teachers and the primary school teachers belong to the same wage group.

The interview with the head teacher revealed that the whole school is included in various projects that require further CPD of professional staff, that they organise common training for all professionals and that they can choose extra training outside the school and according to their wishes. However, he added that staff did not have a strong wish for this kind of training. He believed that this was the result of them being overburdened and also some bad experiences in study groups outside of the school. At the school level, professional staff regularly met in working groups for teachers of certain grades to plan and discuss professional questions. Critical reflection and self-evaluation also took place in working groups, although the head teacher always questions whether the staff are really critical and professional. He also stressed that preschool teachers have brought a new quality into primary schools, because they know much more about six year olds and their needs. He added that parents accepted preschool teachers well, as they enable an easier transition from preschool to primary. The parents wished to keep the everyday contact with professional staff that they had during preschool. Unfortunately, this was not always possible, as some primary school teachers were more sensitive to the interruptions that occur when parents come into the classroom and ask questions.

We collected data in the first grade, where a preschool teacher and a primary school teacher, both with more than 20 years of working experience and both qualified at the higher education level (ISCED 6), were present. In Slovenia, the salaries of preschool teachers and primary school teachers are the same, since the salary of public officials depends on the level of completed education. The preschool teacher had been working in the first grade of primary school for ten years. The primary school teacher worked in first grade every third year, because she stayed with the same group of children for the first three grades of primary school. Therefore, the preschool teacher had to collaborate every year with a different primary school teacher. Primary school and preschool teachers argued that since they were involved in many innovation projects, they had a need for various forms of in-service training. They participated together (as a tandem) only in training and workshops from the Step by Step Network. Through classroom observation, we found evidence that the primary school teachers focused on academic issues and preschool teachers on non-academic issues. According to their answers, they had not developed the habit of reflecting and discussing together their practice; they just exchanged some very short comments during the process of their work. The primary school teacher said that she conducted an analysis educational process every Friday with the children, but this kind of analysis was clearly limited and cannot be a substitute for a serious professional reflection. The preschool teacher added that she connects herself more closely to the other preschool teacher, who works in the other first grade class at this school, than to the primary school teacher from her classroom. Both preschool teachers were allies and supported each other. The preschool teacher thought that in primary school it would be necessary to have a greater sense of the children or more knowledge about how to think from the child's point of view and be more flexible. She told us that she notices the differences in what is important to different teachers in the same profession and in different professions and stressed the role of implicit pedagogy in their case and that it was important that their work is not contradictory, because children and parents can feel this right away.

Conclusions

Work in early childhood classrooms is an integrated activity, and in the child's best interest we cannot separate it into education, care, health, eating, resting, etc. In order to implement all those activities in an integrated manner, staff have to have opportunities for analysing, discussing, negotiating, making agreements, planning and coordinating professional issues and the division of labour amongst themselves. This is especially important in Slovenia, as staff have varied different initial training and working experiences, which result in differences among them in terms of understanding and internalising professional knowledge, values and practices. From our case study, we can learn that in different contexts staff face very different conditions in their professional work and continuous professional development. From the interviews, we can conclude that those conditions are even more important for their professional work than the initial preparation.

Despite the fact that there are national regulations that promote professional development for staff, there are large differences in terms of its implementation in practice. School management entities play an extremely important role in this process. In environments where the management supports and arranges conditions for all staff to be involved in many different ways and forms of professional meetings, discussions, exchanges of experiences and understanding in order to build similar professional values and common understanding of what is good for the children, we found the quality of practice to be at a higher level. These findings are in line with the findings of the CoRe study (Urban et al., 2011) and the interdependency of different layers of the ECEC system. The individual teacher cannot carry all of the responsibility for the quality of education and care processes on his/her shoulders. In our case study, we recognised how important the competences of the institutional and team level of the ECEC system are and how much quality leadership and teamwork can support the quality of the education and care processes. Indirectly, these findings also pointed to the role of the inter-institutional level of the ECEC system in processes of building a competent system within the Step by Step Network. In the framework of this network, teachers and schools received professional guidelines on what, where and how to change their practice and support in investigating and implementing different supporting tools for professional reflections. They also have the opportunity to share their experiences with the broader professional community.

Based on observations in the classrooms in schools where leaders support the professionalisation of staff, we found evidence that all staff are involved in interactions in the classroom; they communicated among themselves and with children intensively and they showed respect and appreciation for active participation in events and discussions in the classroom from all adults and all children. The teacher and the assistant also represented a good model for the children for how to interact with one another. Observations in the classrooms also showed that most of the preschool teachers take on the role of having a full/general insight of what is going on in the classroom. At the same time, their assistants (and the preschool teacher in first grade) took on a lot more responsibilities for individual children by meeting individual needs, encouraging and praising individual children, providing help and explanations for individual children, etc. We could say that they took care of individual children, enabling them to learn, and that this is an extremely professional and important role.

As head teachers are in charge of quality in their schools, it is important that they are well prepared for their role. In Slovenia, all head teachers have to be trained at the School for Head Teachers, but according to other sources of data collected on representative samples of head teachers in Slovenia (Vonta, Gril, 2014, p.150), they lack knowledge and practice in the field of educational leadership. That could explain the fact that even when the management is aware of the lack of critical reflection and self-evaluation of practice by staff, they conclude that little can be done about it. Among the reasons for this phenomenon, they mentioned spatial and organisational conditions, overburdening of the staff with so many projects and that there was insufficient motivation for professional development on the part of some professionals at the school. Due to the economic situation, the government has frozen all salaries in public services for several years now, and there are no differences in salaries whether they are doing their job excellently, not so excellently or even badly. At the same time, there are no other mechanisms for rewarding if the work is done well. On account of this, head teachers are in an unenviable situation. According to the national regulation (Pravilnik o napredovanju zaposlenih v vzgoji in izobraževanju, 2002), teachers can achieve a salary grade promotion every three years based on a head teacher's evaluation. Head teachers must evaluate teachers each year on the basis of observations in the classroom and interviews; additionally, they assess some of the teachers' characteristics, like skills in communication, participation in common activities and independence at work on a very general and subjective level, as the criteria and tools they use for evaluation depend on the head teacher. The criteria and evaluation system for teachers' assistants totally depends on the head teacher's criteria. While they continue to evaluate staff each year, due to the economic crisis, they have nothing concrete with which to award them. However, it is still hard to understand why head teachers, who are, according to national regulations, in charge of arranging the conditions for professional development of the professional staff at schools, are not able to reflect on their role in these processes. Only one third of head teachers were interested in being involved in the activities we offered them through the network to improve their evaluation of teachers' work. This is especially problematic in cases where primary school head teachers are in charge of the quality of the professional work of preschool staff due to the organisational solutions in our educational system (preschool unit at a primary school, preschool teacher in first grade of primary school). Those solutions themselves are not bad ones, but there is a need to focus more attention on establishing special professional support for these types of institutions. Those deficits were also confirmed in other research (Vonta & Gril, 2014, p.143) and call for some changes at the governance level of the ECEC system. Sending staff to in-service programmes and training does not provide major changes in practice; staff need to have opportunities and an obligation to implement new knowledge and practices, and time to reflect on and evaluate their practice with other staff under the supervision of a coach or a pedagogical counsellor (Fukkink & Lont, 2007). Those findings are in line with the Eurofound systematic review (Eurofound, 2015) of studies on effects of long-term continuous professional development. Researchers found that interventions integrated into practice through the provision of ongoing staff support, such as pedagogical guidance and coaching in reflection groups (groups where participants reflect on their professional practice), were proven to be effective and that long-term pedagogical support provided to staff in reflection groups was found to be effective in enhancing the quality of ECEC services (Eurofound, 2015, p.41).

In practice, critical reflection is often carried out on a haphazard basis, when the children are resting or even during the professionals' free time, which gives this activity a sense of being unnecessary. Staff do it because they are asked to do so and do not see it as an opportunity for all staff to learn from each other and to improve their practice. This is particularly obvious when highly qualified staff are working together with assistants with low or no qualifications. We must place more emphasis on preparing professionals and assistants for working and sharing with each other and on taking responsibility for teamwork. All staff involved in our case study emphasised the importance of teamwork competences. We observed that preschool teachers who are working in the first grade of primary schools are losing the specifics of their profession (for example, the holistic approach towards a child's development) because there is no teamwork taking place with primary school teachers where they would be able to share and build common knowledge, practices and values through reflection on their practice. It is also obvious that the professional development of Roma teaching assistants will have to change. They need forms of pedagogical guidance where theory and practice are connected, and a focus on teamwork with some professional guidelines is essential.

From our case study, we can conclude that preschool head teachers who were actively engaged in training and pedagogical guidance in the Step by Step Network, together with their staff (teachers and assistants), have a better understanding of their role in CPD and quality improvement. They were able to create better conditions for staff to be involved in self-evaluation and evaluation of the practices of colleagues, in reflective discussions, in professional discussions on quality indicators and in building shared understanding of the main pedagogical concepts. Professional meetings that include preschool teachers and assistants allow them to gain knowledge, experience and professional values, which enable them to be actively involved in professional discussions and reflect on their own practice and change it towards better quality. Without those competences, staff will continue to perform their practice as they have always done.

We are of course aware that a number of other contexts and conditions exist within the practice of our preschool institutions and schools; however, our study enables us to have an insight into problems and successes in the area of professionalism in early childhood education and care in Slovenia.

References

Eurofound (2015). *Working conditions, training of early childhood care workers and quality of services: a systematic review.* Luxembourg: Publications Office of the European Union.

Fukkink, R., & Lont, A. (2007). Does training matter? Meta-analysis and review of caregiver training studies. *Early Childhood Research Quarterly,* 22 (3), 294–311.

ISSA (2010). *Competent educators of the 21st century: principles of quality pedagogy.* Amsterdam: International Step By Step Association.

Kurikulum za vrtce (1999). Ljubljana: Ministrstvo za šolstvo in sport.

Kolektivna pogodba za dejavnost vzgoje in izobraževanja v Republiki Sloveniji (1994). Uradni list RS, št. 52/94, 49/95, 34/96, 45/96 – popr., 51/98, 28/99, 39/99 – ZMPUPR, 39/00, 56/01, 64/01, 78/01 – popr., 56/02, 43/06 – ZKolP, 60/08, 79/11, 40/12 in 46/13). Retrieved from: http://www.pisrs.si/Pis.web/pregledPredpisa?id=KOLP19.

Pravilnik o nadaljnjem izobraževanju in spopolnjevanju strokovnih delavcev v vzgoji in izobraževanju (2004), Uradni list RS, št. 64/04, 83/05, 27/07, 123/08 in 42/09. Retrieved from: http://pisrs.si/Pis.web/pregledPredpisa?id=PRAV5958.

Pravilnik o napredovanju zaposlenih v vzgoji in izobraževanju v nazive, Uradni list RS, 54/2002. Retrieved from: https://www.uradni-list.si/1/content?id=37063.

Strategija izobraževanja Romov v Republiki Sloveniji (2004). Ljubljana: Ministrstvo za šolstvo in šport. Retrieved from: http://www.mss.gov.si/si/delovna_podrocja/razvoj_solstva/projekti/enake_moznosti/.

Urban, M., Vandenbroeck, M., Peeters, J., Lazzari, A., & Van Laere, K. (2011). *Competence requirements for early childhood education and care.* London and Ghent: UEL and UGent.

Vonta, T., & Gril, A. (2014). *Kompetence, potrebne za opravljanje poklica vzgojitelj predšolskih otrok v sodobnem vrtcu: njihova pomembnost in zastopanost v študijskih programih: zaključno poročilo o raziskavi, Naslov temeljnega raziskovalnega projekta: Identifikacija kompetenc, potrebnih za opravljanje določenih poklicev v primerjavi s kompetencami študijskih programov.* Ljubljana: Pedagoški inštitut.

Zakon o organizaciji in financiranju vzgoje in izobraževanja (1994). Uradni list RS, št. 16/07 – uradno prečiščeno besedilo, 36/08, 58/09, 64/09 – popr., 65/09 – popr., 20/11, 40/12 – ZUJF in 57/12 – ZPCP-2D). Retrieved from: http://pisrs.si/Pis.web/pregledPredpisa?id=ZAKO445.

Zakon o vrtcih (1996). Uradni list RS, 12/1996, št. 100/05 – uradno prečiščeno besedilo, 25/08, 98/09 – ZIUZGK, 36/10, 62/10 – ZUPJS, 94/10 – ZIU in 40/12 – ZUJF. Retrieved from: http://pisrs.si/Pis.web/pregledPredpisa?id=ZAKO447.

6

PERSONAL ATTITUDES AND COMPETENCES OF EDUCATORS AS A PREREQUISITE OF PROGRAMME SUCCESS

The case of the 'Where There Are No Preschools' programme

Olaf Żylicz and Ludmiła Rycielska

Introduction

The Comenius Foundation for Child Development is a Polish non-governmental organisation that seeks to equalise life opportunities for children from birth to 10 years. The programme called 'Where There Are No Preschools' (WTANP; pl. *Gdzie nie ma przedszkola, GNP*) was launched in 2002 to address structural educational inequities faced by young children, especially those living in rural areas where unemployment levels were high (sometimes much over 20 per cent). Official Polish statistics showed at the time that overall preschool attendance was below 40 per cent, with less than 20 per cent in rural areas. There were no policies for equalising the educational opportunities for children from socially and cultur-ally neglected areas. Especially in rural areas, partnerships between teachers and parents were scarce. And everywhere else a traditional-teacher oriented curriculum for preschool education dominated (Ogrodzińska, 2015; Rościszewska-Woźniak, 2010; Żylicz & Malinowska, 2012).

Historical and political context

Before 1989 in the Soviet Union and in the entire communist bloc, women were an indispensable source of labour for industry and agriculture. Almost all parents worked outside their homes. Mothers were offered only short maternity leaves. Therefore, there was a strong need for early childhood care services. In Poland, crèches catered for children up to age three. Many factories and collective farms were obliged to have their own crèches. In kindergartens, where children stayed from age three to six, children were meant to learn to interact with other children and get used to daily routines. Children were introduced to the idea of learning, mostly by means of preschool activities in which they had to participate. Despite some educational activities, caring about children's safety and providing a healthy environment was the primary concern. There was no space for discussions with children. The participatory legacy of Janusz Korczak's (CHR, 2009) teaching was turned into an obsolete, buried history. Children were obliged to learn, play and rest according to an imposed army-like time schedule. There was a body discipline, silence and order. The content of the single obligatory curriculum comprised 'inculcation of the ideals of socialist humanism' or 'rational and emotional ties between children and the Fatherland' (Putkiewicz, 1996). It was the first stage of ideological indoctrination. Parents were not welcome to participate, except on specific prearranged days (Kreusler, 1970; Putkiewicz, 1996; Haskova & Saxonberg, 2011).

Preschool teachers and childcare workers were fairly often accidental persons. In Poland there was no university-level training programme for such teachers. Preschool teachers and childcare workers were underpaid and received little public respect for their work. At the time, a study by Szlesyngier-Gralewska (1982) revealed a relatively low level of self-acceptance in teachers compared to other professional groups. It seems likely that preschool teachers would have probably scored even lower.

For the majority of teachers the collapse of the communist regime in 1989 was a particular challenge. They were not equipped either in terms of competences or proper attitudes to help children grow up as citizens of a democratic society. A former 'professionalism', embodied in allegiance to the state-imposed overregulated curriculum, was no longer valid. Teachers carried into the new era some negative attitudes towards the new system, a sense of permanent grievance and autocratic manners while dealing with children (Harkness et al., 2007; Żylicz & Malinowska, 2012).

Especially in the first two years after the collapse of the system, it was natural for the new educational authorities to negate whatever the communists had been promoting, even if it might have been considered still positive and valid (Janowski, 2007). In 1991, local authorities became responsible for running and financing preschool education. Lack of state subsidising of local education turned out to be a huge burden for many communities, especially in rural areas. The communities had very little revenue from shared personal and corporate income taxes remitted to them from the national government (to date, 2015, farmers have not been included in the personal income tax system). An often geographically dispersed population made the situation even more problematic for local authorities. As a result, between 1990 and 1999, almost 30 percent of all preschools were closed (Levitas et al., 2001).

Official framework for preschool education (ECEC from birth to five/six years)

The Act on the Education System of 1991 (WDoE, 2010) serves as a general framework for an entire education system and embodies changes in its ideological bases. It was defined in the context of universal ethical principles, while taking into account Christian heritage. It fosters admiration of the father-land and respect for Polish cultural heritage, as well as openness to values of European and world cultures. The purpose of the school is to enable the com-prehensive development of the student and prepare him/her for family and civil responsibilities.

In Poland, mandatory education covers children aged 6–16 years (Eurydice, 2014). It includes the final year of preschool education, six years primary educa-tion and three years lower-secondary education. Early childhood education and care is provided on two levels: for children under the age of three (in regular crèches or similar daycare settings) and for children aged three–five/six years. Preschool education from age three is offered either in nursery schools or pre-school classes in primary schools and is supervised by the ministry responsible for school education. For children aged three and four, preschool attendance is voluntary.

Five year olds are now required by law to complete a school preparatory year in one of the preschool settings mentioned above. Children who reach the age of six in a given calendar year start their education in a primary school (according to the education system reform in 2014 this is compulsory only for children born in the first half of 2008 and from 2015 – for all six year olds). This is due to the gradual lowering of the age of commencement of compulsory education in primary school from the age of seven to the age of six. The lowering was strongly opposed by influential parents' associations and became a topic of controversial public discus-sion in Poland (Ombudsman for Parents' Rights, 2012). Some parents perceived it as an undesirable intrusion of the state into family life. Most parents of children up to five years were against compulsory schooling for all six year olds (64 percent of all parents; CBOS, 2013). Twenty-nine per cent of parents in rural areas were convinced that home care is better than institutional care, compared with, only 10 percent of residents of the biggest Polish cities (CBOS, 2013).

Teacher education and training standards were formulated in a recent regula-tion by the Ministry of Science and Higher Education (MSHE, 2012). Teacher education and training consists of preparation in a given subject matter (biology, mathematics, etc.) and pedagogical training (i.e. teaching methods, psychol-ogy, pedagogy). Under the regulation, teachers employed in pre-primary and primary schools ought to have a bachelor's degree as a minimum qualification, whereas teachers employed in lower-secondary and upper-secondary schools as well as basic vocational schools ought to hold, at the minimum, a master's degree or equivalent.

Professional responsibilities and entailments of teachers are defined in the Teachers' Charter (pl. *Karta Nauczyciela*; e.g. WEDoE, 2010), an official legal state-ment, dating back to communist times. Besides teachers' entitlements it defines the required qualifications and professional advancement path (Eurydice, 2012).

The official national *Core Curriculum for Preschool Education in Kindergartens and Preschool Sections in Primary Schools* was initially introduced in February 2002 and then amended six years later. It was expected to become a milestone in professionalisation in preschool teaching. The curriculum goals of preschool education are, among others, as follows:

- developing children's talents;
- shaping intellectual skills necessary for both everyday life functioning and further education;
- directing children towards moral sensitivity;
- developing social skills and emotional resistance;
- developing self expression;
- shaping a sense of belonging to diverse communities;
- supporting children's curiosity, activity and independence.

(MNE, 2008)

The curriculum also defines activities of teachers and preschool children. They comprise four complementary domains:

1. acquisition of knowledge and understanding of oneself and the world;
2. acquisition of skills through activities;
3. building bonds with peer groups and community;
4. advancement of the system of values and personal standards.

(Eurydice, 2010)

The national Core curriculum serves as the basis and reference point for the preparation of a preschool's curriculum by teachers. All institutions offering any forms of preschool education are obliged to follow their curricula after they are approved by the preschool head and consulted with teachers and parents. The curriculum proposes splitting children's total time in preschool as follows: one fifth of the time to be devoted to play, one fifth to outdoor activities, one fifth to educational activities and the rest to care and organisational tasks. Most preschools open for about nine hours a day (the minimum opening time for preschools in primary schools is five hours per day) and five days a week (Eurydice, 2014).

Preschool teachers are responsible for systematic observation of children and for keeping records of their progress to better understand their needs, and to cooperate with other specialists or parents. The curriculum makes teachers of five and six year olds responsible for the assessment of preschool children's readiness for primary-school education. The parents of a child at the end of the preschool education receive a written document informing them about the readiness (Eurydice, 2005).

Educational provision in most preschool institutions is organised on the basis of the age of children (Eurydice, 2014). The number of children in one class should not exceed 25. Usually two teachers working in shifts take care of one class. There are no official requirements pertaining to teaching methods. Some institutions create or adopt methods related to certain methodological and pedagogical approaches, e.g. the Montessori paradigm or the Comenius Foundation approach, described below. Preschool teachers are mostly female – around 99 percent of teachers at the preschool level (Eurydice, 2008).

Only recently have state education authorities begun to analyse the quality of preschool education in depth and systematically. The Ministry of National Education, accompanied by two country-wide educational institutions (MNE, ORE & IBE, 2014), proposed new standards for assessing the quality of services provided in preschools. They defined relevant formal and informal indices, which go significantly beyond current rather vague general statements on the subject matter. The tangible indices imply: number of children per square metre, number of children per qualified practitioner, number of hours spent with a qualified practitioner, and – which appears very fresh and new – the use of diagnosis and observation information. In turn the intangible ones were named as setting challenges and adequate support, spending quality time and offering attention and quality of space and amenities.

WTANP: programme principles and changes

WTANP was implemented in over one hundred rural communities with 170 teachers directly involved. Most of these communities offered no other preschool education services. The programme was meant to be as educationally, organisationally and financially effective as possible. Regular full-time preschool education (five to nine hours per day/five week days) suited neither rural children's families nor the financial resources of the local authorities. Therefore, the number of hours a child spent on the WTANP programme was nine per week. Teachers were specially trained to work at WTANP centres. Both democratic, trust-based and coaching-type attitudes, and varied interpersonal and educational skills, were trained and monitored, which made the programme unique but also often a subject of reproach from the mainstream educational system (Żylicz, 2010).

WTANP draws on child-centred approaches to early education. These approaches have had a long tradition, from Comenius through Locke, Rousseau, Pestalozzi, Fröbel, Montessori, Dalton, Isaacs and Anna Freud to Lilian Katz – the contemporary US early childhood education and child development expert of worldwide renown. WTANP uses an early education approach, which emphasizes learning through exploration and play, observational behaviour modelling, creative activities, teachers' sensitive receptivity and parental involvement. At the same time, the Comenius Foundation embraces in its programmes significant cultural factors. This is why WTANP is an ever-growing effort, combining local contexts (relations with local authorities and local people's socioeconomic situations, especially in communities where state-owned farms used to operate under the previous communist system) with the professional qualifications and dispositions of the WTANP teachers.

WTANP: a competent system

The WTANP project has been a challenge to all formal educational services that are founded on hierarchical and rigidly governed by 'top down' educational processes. WTANP treats the education of the youngest children as a system based on mutual respect between teachers, parents and local communities. Whenever the balance, real commitment and mutual cooperation occur among these three groups involved in a given WTANP centre the programme proved to be beneficial for the children involved. In other words, this entire entity is treated as an educationally competent system, capable of defining directions, jointly running the centres and offering feedback information necessary to evaluate the quality of provision.

The situation of WTANP has changed since the introduction of the law *Other Forms of Preschool Education* (2008). For the first time since its inception, WTANP, which until then was treated as an alternative educational system, gained the status of 'real education' in the rural areas. This was a victory for the high quality of educational centres and clubs, as well as other forms of activities of nongovernmental organisations. The Comenius Foundation was instrumental in this legal change. It proved to be easier to convince the Polish government and the politicians than to overcome resistance of ZNP (*Związek Nauczycielstwa Polskiego* [Polish Teachers' Union]) and the teachers of public traditional preschools, who felt threatened by these initiatives and saw these actions as undermining their position and the quality of education, as they tended to understand it.

The above-mentioned legal changes enabled registration of forms of education for children from three–five years of age that differ from the mainstream model. Many local authorities (over 70 percent) that were involved in WTANP and other similar projects registered the clubs and centres as official preschool facilities and centres. Some of the mentioned facilities function as community centres, while others (10–20 percent) as private institutions managed by nongovernmental associations and, in a few cases, as companies owned by the teachers.

After 2008 coordinators of WTANP faced the critical dilemma of whether or not to join the official educational system (see Table 6.1). Quality, efficiency, but also the permanency of the programme were at stake.

WTANP: the case for a specific professional qualification

The majority of teachers (about 90 per cent) who want to enter WTANP have formal academic qualifications (on preschool education). However, this background does not provide the competences required from WTANP teachers. They are sufficiently good at pedagogical theory, basics of didactics and planning. But they do not have enough practice, knowledge and understanding of child psychology, lack the ability to solve everyday problems and have little experience of cooperating with parents and the local environment.

Specific WTANP training comprises at least 60 hours, sometimes (financial resources allowing) up to 100 hours. The training comprises, among other things:

• Constructing curriculum: taking into consideration the educational environment, observational data, understanding and tracking child development;

TABLE 6.1 Pros and cons of WTANP operating centres within the official education system from the perspective of local communities

	WTANP in the education system	WTANP outside the education system
Advantages for the community	Possibility to apply for European grants from the educational programmes. Supervision from the Ministry of Education.	Better possibilities to adjust to the needs of the local society. Possibility to use a variety of non-educational funding. More responsibility for the quality of education, especially if the hosting community is involved and committed.
Disadvantages for the community	Obligation to employ teachers according to the Teachers' Charter, which implies strict rules and larger costs.	Need to find funding for sustaining the quality of work. WTANP will be able to include only children between three–four years of age, because the older ones will be subject to obligatory education.

- Building proper relationships with children – the future WTANP teachers train: listening and communication skills; helping children to become more and more independent, confident, capable of solving diverse problems; and coping with the freedom of the individual in the social environment. The teachers also learn how to talk with children when they misbehave, mostly by means of contracts;
- Cooperation with parents – covers: engaging parents; adequate and effective communication; development of openness on parental expertise; and solving interpersonal problems;
- Educational environment: as these teachers are going to be leaders of change, they must learn how to cope with often unfavourable environment, how to build social support for the undertaken actions by cooperation or communication with local government units, schools, councils etc.

Additionally, the teachers receive 30 hours of in-service training each year, plus opportunities to benefit from cooperation with WTANP consultants and mentors. In order to maintain the high quality of WTANP centres and unceasing development of teachers' competences an original system of mentoring has been introduced. It is a major form of support for the WTANP teachers in practice. Initializing and supporting the motivation of teachers to develop professionally is critical for the WTANP mentoring approach. Twenty-four mentors have been working for WTANP in Poland. Some of them were treated as senior, fully-fledged mentors and others, most often teachers, are called tutors but the senior ones supervise their work. The entire group of mentors has common meetings every half a year. In 2009 over 250 mentor meetings with teachers took place across all the WTANP centres (Ogrodzińska, 2015; Rosciszewska-Woźniak, 2010; Żylicz, 2007, 2010).

Development goals of WTANP

The programme was meant foremost to develop four major competences the WTANP children are to acquire while in the centres: self-confidence, social competence, persistence and interest/curiosity. This makes the programme absolutely unique in Poland as a real focus on these competences goes far beyond the goals in the mainstream early childhood sector (like writing or reading skills). Nonetheless they look very congruent with the ones defined in the aforementioned official CoRe curriculum. We believe – based on long experience of educators of the Comenius Foundation – that the acquisition of these competences is a prerequisite for advancement of all other academic competences. Those who graduate from WTANP face a big challenge while transitioning from highly democratic and participatory centres to state-run primary schools, which are still fairly hierarchical and operate on the principle of compliance and order, and sometimes require fewer cognitive demands.

Furthermore, the mentioned competences of children are also a kind of benchmark for all other stakeholders involved in education in WTANP centres, that is teachers, parents and, to some degree, even representatives of local communities. The WTANP teachers are to teach, nurture and foster these competencies, but foremost they must be role models for the children. In other words, the quality of their work is first assessed against these competences (Żylicz, 2007, 2010). The teachers are expected to operate as educational tutors fostering children's development in a highly individualised way (Brzezińska & Rycielska, 2009).

WTANP competences explained

Self-confidence is understood as an outward manifestation of psychological strength, especially in situations that are new or difficult to handle. It can be learnt to some degree in the process of behaviour training or modelling. Self-confidence is accompanied by the belief that '*I am worth loving*', '*I deserve acceptance and respect*' or '*I am competent.*'

For children from rural areas the development of self-confidence is particularly difficult for two reasons. Firstly, adult–child relations in Polish rural communities have, for centuries, been strongly hierarchichical. Children's socialisation has usually been equated with satisfying adults' expectations. Therefore, self-confidence may be seen as the exact opposite of obedience – a desirable characteristic from the point of view of traditional parenting and schooling (Harkness et al., 2007).

Social competence (also: social-emotional skills or socio-moral skills) (Katz & McClellan, 1997) is an umbrella term given to many skills that facilitate friendly and effective interactions with others. Children should develop an understanding of interaction rules and standards to behave in acceptable – and different – ways towards other children during play and towards teachers in classroom settings. The key is to understand other people's needs and to be able to adopt their perspectives. This can be done on a more emotional level, when a child is sad because another child is sad, or on a more cognitive level, when a child can intellectually grasp and articulate another child's problem.

Most rural children are in a position of advantage here, as they have much more opportunity for informal social interaction with their peers and adults other than parents or carers on a daily basis than urban children, who spend a great deal of time attending classes, private lessons and travelling separately to and from school.

Interest/curiosity is the psychological need to seek information and interaction with one's environment (physical environment and other people). From birth we pay attention to new phenomena around us. The key to children's future academic achievement is to encourage their intellectual interest and to help them develop regular working habits (Von Stumm, et al., 2011). In Poland, mainstream education philosophy continues to be based mostly on a reproduction of information. This often weakens the child's disposition to be captivated by reality and the need to explore it. In a large US study, a great majority of teachers found digital technologies creating an "easily distracted generation with short attention spans" and around two thirds believe they "do more to distract students than to help them academically" (Purcell et al., 2012). Therefore long-term curiosity development is endangered. Paradoxically, in relatively poorer rural areas where WTANP centres have been operating, it has been easier to inspire interest and curiosity in children. The programme children usually have had fewer opportunities than average urban children and those from more affluent rural areas, to directly interact with real objects of culture and civilization, including new technological devices. Enthusiasm, commitment and a highly personalized approach from the programme teachers seem critically instrumental in fostering curiosity to enable them to transgress the boundaries of often very limited social and academic experience of their parents (Żylicz, 2007).

Persistence is the ability to continue in spite of distractions (Yeager et al., 2014). Persistence in pursuing one's goals is a prerequisite for success (sporting, academic or business achievement). It is closely connected with the disposition to stay focused on a task, giving it one's undivided attention. Difficulties in concentration are connected with a very high speed of response reaction to internal and external stimuli that keep distracting the child (Kuśpit, 2002). Persistence and interest go hand in hand. It is much easier to bring a difficult task to completion if one is motivated by natural curiosity and interest in seeing that problem solved.

WTANP teachers encourage children's persistence by showing faith in their final success, by telling them that they expect them to complete their tasks, by not rewarding children until they have finished their work, by praising those who have put in some extra effort, by teaching children how to rephrase a question that seems too difficult to tackle and by showing them how to start again.

Systematic and continuous evaluation of WTANP practice

To increase the quality of early education in Poland the Comenius Academy has been established and its Training Centre (27 trainers) offers training for more than 1,300 teachers per year. The Comenius Foundation has set very high standards for professionalising the work of all teachers attending any of its programmes. It offers both preparatory and in service training in special workshops fitted to the teachers needs. It regularly uses *Reflective Professional* – a survey form for teachers with open questions concerning the pedagogical work that enables self-reflection, self-evaluation and self-improvement. Furthermore, mentors trained by the Foundation offer permanent mentoring services, which is a freely agreed alliance between mentors and teachers based on trust, responsibility for the changes on the teacher side, confidentiality, the reflection on the process of the changes: reflection, observation, discussion and action plans. Regular evaluations of the quality of centres are provided by teachers themselves, by parents who are encouraged to be present in the classrooms, by local authorities and, to some degree, also by children as evaluations are expected to cover relevant children's narratives. All parties involved – that is parents, teachers and local authorities – jointly analyse the actions of the preschool centre according to the standards and identify areas for further improvement or development. They are invited to take responsibility for the high quality of the provision in primary schools at large. The teachers and representatives of local authorities are regularly invited by the Comenius Foundation to attend workshops and conferences for both educational purposes but also to make their voices heard outside their local communities (Ogrodzińska, 2015; Rościszewska-Woźniak, 2010; Żylicz, 2010).

A pilot project of Certificating Preschool Centres was successfully launched in 16 centres. To a large extent, the project is based on internal permanent self-evaluation in order to maintain and improve the quality of the provision (Rościszewska-Woźniak, 2010).

In order to establish whether the programme was working as expected, a large-scale, external evaluation was commissioned in 2007. Educational programmes are often criticised for being ineffective, or more accurately, we rarely understand links between educational provision and changes in children (Żylicz, 2007). Moreover, we usually know nothing about the financial effectiveness of such programmes and there are often many challenges to be faced while running such evaluations: giving proper weight to the psychological criteria under examination vs. teachers–students relations, taking into account the values on which a given programme is founded, considering all stakeholders and wider context (e.g., educational policy). We assumed, after Fleischman and Williams (1996), that no evaluation can be considered successful unless its findings are employed to make genuine improvements in education, enhancing children's chances for academic achievement.

As early as 2004 the Comenius Foundation commissioned a study to find out how WTANP graduates were achieving in primary school reception classes compared to children who had attended preschool and those who had not (CFCD,

2004). Teachers were asked to complete questionnaires about their children's school readiness. The questionnaire contained 33 statements about skills that facilitated school adjustment (teamwork, memorisation of nursery rhymes, proper emotional expression, etc.).

The study involved a total of 281 children in primary school reception classes; 50 of had previously attended regular preschool, 98 had attended the WTANP programme and 133 children had not attended any kind of preschool service. A larger number of children who had attended regular preschool were found to have above-average school-adjustment competencies than WTANP graduates (38 per cent versus 27 per cent). Both groups, however, were far better skilled than children without preschool experience (a mere 3 per cent of them were judged to be above-average in this respect). It should be noted, however, that most of the WTANP children had attended WTANP sessions only for three hours a day and only three days a week, which is a far shorter attendance period than that offered by regular preschool establishments.

The major assessment was carried out between September 2006 and February 2007 (Żylicz, 2007). The evaluation project was designed to look at children's behaviour from four basic perspectives that, as stated before, the Foundation has identified as key early-childhood development competences. These four categories were assessed with evaluation instruments, i.e. questionnaires (Children's Behaviour Questionnaire for parents (CBQ-P) and for teachers (CBQ-T)) and interviews. A longitudinal design was not possible due to financial and time constraints.

The survey phase of the project involved mainly comparing a representative sample of WTANP graduates in primary school reception classes with their peers who had not used a regular preschool education service. In total 189 children were assessed: including 41 who filled out an additional locus of control scale (the number of WTANP and non-WTANP children was comparable). Locus of control refers to the extent to which investigated children believe they are personally responsible for effects of their behaviour, be it successes or failures. Internal locus of control, a generalised belief that one's life is primarily determined by his/her own actions, is an important personal cognitive resource helping future success (Żylicz, 2010).

Assessment by means of questionnaires was carried out by reception-class teachers in state-run schools that had no connection with the WTANP programme. These comparisons were crucial, as they focused on children's behaviour in new settings (with new children around) and with new requirements ahead, showing the robustness of the competences under the training in WTANP centres.

To confirm the data collected from teachers the descriptions provided by the children's parents were also considered. The above-mentioned questionnaires were complemented by focus group interviews with reception-class teachers, WTANP teachers and parents of WTANP children. The qualitative data allowed us to develop a better understanding of the correlations revealed in the quantitative measures.

Key findings

According to parents, WTANP graduates had higher ratings in each developmental area surveyed than children without preschool education. According to the teachers these correlations were less obvious in school settings. The teachers reported the most significant differences in the levels of self-confidence and, to some extent, in the levels of curiosity. In their focus group interviews, however, teachers emphasised gains in social competence (in WTANP graduates).

Significantly, WTANP graduates had higher scores in the locus of control questionnaire, which they had completed with the help of the evaluators. This finding is important in the context of their future emotional and social development. Unlike other children without preschool education, these children felt more responsible for the events in their lives, especially for their own achievements (Żylicz, 2010).

Additionally, analyses were carried out on the findings of the Children's Behaviour Questionnaire (completed by teachers) for children in five groups: children in primary school reception classes (as described above, WTANP graduates and children without preschool education), current WTANP beneficiaries aged five to six, and matched preschoolers from small and large towns. Current WTANP beneficiaries proved to have significantly higher ratings than reception-class children without preschool education on each of the four categories surveyed, and significantly higher ratings than WTANP graduates in reception classes on two categories: interest/curiosity and social competence. The latter result suggests that these two competences of WTANP graduates deteriorate in regular schools. In turn, current WTANP beneficiaries did not differ from the other two comparison groups, namely preschoolers in large towns and preschoolers in small towns (but it should be remembered WTANP children had substantially fewer weekly provision hours).

It is worth mentioning that internal, although rather informal reports on the practice of WTANP teachers are systematically being carried out. These reports show a huge diversity of attitudes towards children and teaching among the WTANP teachers. Some of them, despite extensive training provided by the Foundation, still tend to behave in a fairly directed way, not excluding punishments as a form of regulating behaviour of children. Such an approach, which we found in a small minority of WTANP centres, resembles more the autocratic methods of the past than the approach propagated by the Foundation (FRD, 2008; Rościszewska-Woźniak, 2010; Żylicz, 2007, 2010).

Once teachers were asked by means of internal survey (FRD, 2008) to write what kind of benefits they have from being part of WTANP. Quotes from some of the statements provided highlight the WTANP experience from the perspective of the teachers and provide insight into the advancement of attitudes and competences under consideration.

I have started to look differently at my own children.

Previously I was afraid to have supervisory visits when I work with kids, now with ongoing presence of parents with us I am much braver in this respect.

I have a sense of doing important things.

New methods of work have been a great challenge to me.

The year I have been in WTANP I learned what is precious in myself and I am sharing it with my children in the centre.

I was moved and happy when we had a visitation from Warsaw. Other teachers of the traditional educational system were surprised I liked the situation. But I have had a feeling my friends have come to help me.

The most critical thing to me is that in the centre we all feel equally important.

General conclusions

In spite of its limited timeframe (usually nine hours per week), WTANP has had a notable and mainly positive impact on its young beneficiaries, and a considerable impact on their teachers and families too (as indicated by focus group interviews). In this respect, the most valuable data comes from teachers teaching WTANP graduates in primary school reception classes. In general, reception-class teachers had positive perceptions, which they voiced in their interviews and questionnaires. These positive perceptions are especially valuable, considering that many of those teachers are used to a much more authoritarian style, with strongly hierarchical teacher–student relations – in contrast to WTANP centres, where teachers are expected to follow rather than direct the child.

The most salient question involves the challenges that WTANP graduates face on transition to primary school reception classes of mainstream, traditionally run schools. Differences in ratings between current WTANP beneficiaries (higher levels of interest and social skills) and WTANP graduates in primary school reception classes (who should be developmentally more mature and therefore more advanced in every category surveyed, i.e. persistence, social competence, interest and self-confidence), as well as data from teacher interviews suggest that difficulties encountered by WTANP children on transition to the regular school system must be addressed. The data collected raised an important question: How can these high ratings, especially high ratings on interest and social skills, be maintained on transition to primary school? This question is related to another one: How can WTANP graduates be helped to adjust to a different set of requirements and to a more traditional approach to teacher–student relations, prevalent in many school settings?

The findings (for primary school reception classes) turned out to be ambiguous in respect of *social competence*. WTANP graduates were rated higher on socialisation only in interviews and in questionnaires completed by parents, even though the development of children's social skills is high on the programme's agenda. Some reception-class teachers cited WTANP graduates' *self-confidence* as a source of trouble. This is understandable: teachers in quite traditional rural communities are used to higher levels of subordination and reactive behaviour in the classroom. At the same time, heightened self-confidence is valuable in itself, and may translate into children's future success at school and in life.

As regards *interest* and *persistence*, it was found desirable to introduce some more routine activities (teacher-directed experiences) into the programme to help five year olds to get used to 'that boring school stuff'. It does not seem to be a widespread problem, but some of the WTANP graduates do find it difficult to engage in teacher-planned tasks. At the same time, natural curiosity and perseverance – just like self-confidence – increase WTANP children's chances of continuing their education past the school-leaving age.

Additionally, an independent internal survey carried out in 2008 in six WTANP localities on determinants of high quality education in WTANP centres confirms the approach. Six relevant required categories have been recurrently mentioned in this research (FRD, 2008):

- A programme with clear pedagogical assumptions;
- Professional teachers;
- Positive interpersonal relations within the preschool centre;
- Cooperation between teachers and parents;
- Good work conditions for the preschool centre;
- Cooperation with the local community.

Final remarks

Let us look towards the end at WTANP in the perspectives of CoRe (Urban et al,, 2011). WTANP has proved to be a successful programme. Since its inception in 2002 it has come a very long way. From a very modest, small-scale educational endeavour outside of the mainstream it has developed into an influential programme across the country. At the same time experts from the Comenius Foundation have had a substantial impact on early childhood education legislation and have defined and implemented countrywide relevant standards, both for early childhood education and care (ECEC) and its teachers. The selection and training of open-minded, proactive, democratic teachers, eager to acquire and unfold new competences, and humble about receiving permanent feedback, was key to the success. They are treated by the Comenius Foundation and they mostly operate, as self-reliant, trusted, capable and accountable subjects, whose foremost task is to inspire children and show them how to systematically and creatively strive for their personal interests and passions in harmony with others. Teachers' competences are as much and no more than just tools in the course of accompanying children in this educational journey. Teachers are usually very proud of working for the programme and aware that it helps building a better position for ECEC teachers in the country, despite – sometimes very fierce – resistance from the mainstream educational institutions and their traditionally minded representatives.

WTANP as a system of knowledge and practice is permanently created and re-created within a community of children, teachers, parents and local authorities. The Comenius Foundation sets standards and development directions, offers democratic type supervision and shares tools for unceasing self-improvement. In all that uniqueness

WTANP remains a positive challenge for the Polish overregulated and often undemocratic education system at large.

References

Brzezińska, A.I., & Rycielska, L. (2009). Tutoring jako czynnik rozwoju ucznia i nauczyciela [Tutoring as a factor of students and teachers development]. In: P. Czekierda, M. Budzynski, J. Traczynski, Z. Zalewski, & A. Zembrzuska (eds.), *Tutoring w szkole* [Tutoring at school]. Wrocław: Towarzystwo Edukacji Otwartej, pp. 19–30.

CBOS (2013). *Czy sześciolatki powinny pójść do szkoły?* [Should 6-years-olds go to school?]. Warsaw: CBOS. Retrieved from: http://www.cbos.pl/SPISKOM. POL/2013/K_090_13.PDF.

CFCD (2004) Report. Retrieved from: http://www.frd.org.pl.

CHR/Commissioner for Human Rights (2009). *Janusz Korczak: The Child's Right to Respect – Janusz Korczak's Legacy Lectures on Today's Challenges for Children*. Strasbourg: Council of Europe Publishing.

Eurydice (2005). *Report Prepared for Structure of Education, Vocational Training and Adult Education Systems in Europe*. Brussels: Eurydice, CEDEFOP and ETF.

Eurydice (2008). *The System of Education in Poland*. Brussels: Eurydice. Retrieved from: http://eurydice.org.pl/wp-content/uploads/2014/10/the_system_2008.pdf.

Eurydice (2010). *The System of Education in Poland*. Brussels: Eurydice. Retrieved from: http://www.eurydice.org.pl/sites/eurydice.org.pl/files/the_system_2010.pdf.

Eurydice (2012). *The System of Education in Poland*. Brussels: Eurydice. Retrieved from: http://www.frse.org.pl/sites/frse.org.pl/files/publication/1273/system-education-poland.pdf.

Eurydice (2014). *The System of Education in Poland*. Warsaw: Eurydice. Retrieved from: http://eurydice.org.pl/wp/content/uploads/2014/10/THE-SYSTEM_2014_www.pdf.

Fleischman, H., & Williams, L. (1996). *An Introduction to Program Evaluation for Classroom Teachers*. Arlington, VA: Development Associates.

FRD (2008). *Oceny GNP oczami nauczycieli programu* [Programme teachers evaluate WTANP]. Warsaw: FRD.

Haskova, H., & Saxonberg, S. (2011). The institutional roots of post-communist family policy: comparing the Czech and Slovak republics. In: F. Mackay and M. L. Krook (eds.), *Gender, Politics, and Institutions: Towards a Feminist Institutionalism*. Basingstoke: Palgrave Macmillan, pp. 112–128.

Harkness, S., Blom, M., Oliva, A., Moscardino, U., Żylicz, P.O., Rios Bermudez. M. et al. (2007). Teachers' ethnotheories of the "ideal student" in five western cultures. *Comparative Education*, 43, 1: 113–135.

Janowski, A. (2007). Educational restructuring and change: post-educational transformation in Poland. *ORBIS SCHOLAE*, 1, 2: 80–109.

Katz, L. & McClellan, D. (1997). *Fostering Children's Social Competence: The Teacher's Role*. Washington, D.C.: National Association for the Education of Young Children.

Kreusler, A. (1970). Soviet preschool education. *The Elementary School Journal*, 70, 8: 429–437.

Kuśpit, M. (2002). Wpływ temperamentu na zaburzenia w zachowaniu dzieci i młodzieży. [Influence of temperament on disturbed behavior in children and adolescents]. *Annales*, vol. XV, section J. Wydawnictwo UMCS, Lublin, 123–141.

Lamb M.E., Sternberg K.J., Hwang C.P., Broberg A.G. (1992). *Child Care in Context: Crosscultural Perspectives*. Hillsdale NJ: Lawrence Erlbaum.

Levitas, A., Golinowska, S., & Herczynski, J. (2001). *Improving Rural Education in Poland: Report Prepared for the Warsaw Delegation of the European Commission*. Warsaw: CASE Foundation.

MNE (2008). *Rozporządzenie Ministra Edukacji Narodowej z dnia 23 grudnia 2008 r w sprawie podstawy programowej wychowania przedszkolnego oraz kształcenia ogólnego w poszczególnych typach szkół* [Ordinance of the Minister of National Education of CoRe curriculum for preschool education in kindergartens and preschool sections in primary schools of 23rd December 2008 on core curriculum for preschool education in kindergartens and pre-school sections in primary schools]. Warsaw: MNE.

MNE, ORE, IBE (2014). Wysoka jakość edukacji przedszkolnej [High quality of preschool education]. Cracow: conference.

MSHE (2012). *Rozporządzenie Ministra Nauki i Szkolnictwa Wyższego z dnia 17 stycznia 2012 r. w sprawie standardów kształcenia przygotowującego do wykonywania zawodu nauczyciela* [Ordinance of the Minister of Science and Higher Education on 17th January 2012 on standards for education preparing teachers]. Warsaw: MSHE.

Ogrodzińska, T. (2015). "Gdy nie ma przedszkoli": wprowadzenie zmiany społecznej przez organizacje pozarządowe [WTANP: an introduction of the social change by the NGO]. *Psychologia Wychowawcza*, 7: 181–204.

Ombudsman for Parents' Rights (2012). *Report: Warunki edukacji przedszkolnej* [Underpinnings of preschool education]. Retrieved from: http://www.rzecznikrodzicow.pl/sites/default/files/raport_edukacja_przedszkolna_calosc.pdf. Warsaw: Ombudsman for Parents' Rights.

Purcell, K., Rainie, L., Heaps, A., Buchanan, J., Friedrich, L., Jacklin, A., et al. (2012). How teens do research in the digital world. *Pew Internet Project*. Washington: Pew Research Center.

Putkiewicz, E. (1996). *Culture and the Kindergarten Curriculum in Poland*. Paper presented at the European Conference on the Quality of Early Childhood Education (6th, Lisbon, Portugal, September 1–4, 1996).

Rościszewska-Woźniak, M. (2010). Improving kindergarten and pre- primary education accessibility in rural areas: experience of Poland. Vilnius: conference.

Szlesyngier-Gralewska, J. (1982). Structure of didactic activity and teacher's self-acceptance, *Psychologia Wychowawcza*, 25, 1: 39–50.

Urban, M., Vandenbroeck, M., Peeters, J., Lazzari, A., & Von Laere, K. (2011). *Competence Requirements in Early Childhood Education and Care*: CoRe Final Report Brussels: European Commission.

Von Stumm, S., Hell, B., Chamorro-Premuzic, T. (2011). The hungry mind: intellectual curiosity is the third pillar of academic performance. *Perspectives on Psychological Science*, 6, 6: 574–588.

WDoE (2012). *World Data on Education*. Poland: UNESCO Retrieved from: http://www.ibe.unesco.org/fileadmin/user_upload/Publications/WDE/2010/pdf-versions/Poland.pdf.

Yeager, D.S., Henderson, M., Paunesku, D., Walton, G.M., D'Mello, S., Spitzer, B.J., et al. (2014). Boring but important: a self-transcendent purpose for learning fosters academic self-regulation. *Journal of Personality and Social Psychology*, 107, 4: 559–580.

Żylicz, P.O. (2007). The Evaluation of Where There Are No Preschools Program. Warsaw: report.

Żylicz, P.O. (2010). Where there are no preschools: an educational program fostering self-efficacy in Polish rural areas. In: A. Tuna, & J. Hayden (eds.), *Early Childhood Programs as the Doorway to Social Cohesion: Application of Vygotsky's Ideas from an East-West Perspective*. Cambridge: Cambridge Scholars Publishing, pp. 17–30.

Żylicz, P.O., & Malinowska, D. (2012). Report: Przygotowanie polskich eksperymentalnych wersji skal samo opisowych dla nauczycieli. [Experimental self-assessment scales for teachers]. Warsaw.

7

THE EARLY YEARS PROFESSIONAL IN ENGLAND

Claire Cameron and Linda Miller

Introduction

This chapter reviews and critiques the development of a national model of professionalisation in England, namely the Early Years Professional (EYP). The EYP was introduced following consultation in 2005 and was replaced in 2013 by a new model, the Early Years Teacher (EYT). The chapter considers approaches to addressing the question of improving the 'competence' and professional status of the early childhood education and care (ECEC) workforce.

This chapter documents the rise and fall of the EYP model, which developed during a period of unprecedented investment in and expansion of the ECEC sector. This initiative was one of a series of attempts to resolve long-term problems with the early childhood workforce, which had been characterised by a conceptual split between 'care' oriented occupations such as nursery worker and 'education' models such as teacher.

Describing what early childhood workers do and how good they have to be at it – their competence – becomes an ever more intricate task. Looking at the topic from a cross-national perspective the task of describing or assessing competence is even more complex as it is embedded in a country's values about children and childhood, and its aims for early childhood services. The debate about competence is important for two reasons. First, a competent workforce is fundamental to the quality of provision. Many studies agree that where centres have staff with higher level qualifications they also have a more stimulating and supportive environment for children and better developmental outcomes (OECD 2006; Urban et al. 2011). Competence and higher-level initial qualifications are intimately linked.

Second, the debate about competence is about how practice is thought about and conducted. In England (and in other English-speaking countries), the debate is largely driven by an understanding that competence is about performance to pre-scribed levels or standards. It is about 'can-do aspects of learning, arguably to the detriment of knowledge, understanding and all round development' (McKenzie et al. 1995: preface). By contrast, in many continental European countries, com-petence has a more nuanced and developmental meaning, referring not just to knowledge or skills, but also the ability to successfully meet complex demands in a particular context (OECD 2005). With this distinction in mind, English policy and practice is likely to be evaluated in terms of competent as 'good enough' practice according to preset and external ideals of what that is (Cameron 2011).

The chapter is in four parts. First, we give an overview of the wider context for early childhood education in England, including a discussion of recent policy-led developments. Second, we offer an account of the development of the EYP role. Third we discuss the replacement of EYP Status with the recent introduction of EYTs. Fourthly, we return to issues of context, and offer a critique of where issues of competence and professionalisation of the early childhood education and care workforce is heading in England.

Overall, there has been a slow shift towards recognition of the importance of formal training and education for ECEC work in all settings, so that today virtually all scholars in the field agree that early childhood work is complex and requires a high level of formal education (Oberhümer 2000). Some major barriers to pursuing this are: first, the ECEC field is not united behind a single concept or organisa-tional body. Various representative bodies had different ideas about the purpose of provision. Was it to support the labour market, to provide substitute mothers or to care and educate? A lack of unity hampered a single route to professionalisation. Second, despite the findings of powerful studies around appropriate knowledge for ECEC work, policy makers preferred pragmatic solutions and found ways of 'trad-ing up' qualifications while disrupting the system of provision, dominated by the private market, as little as possible.

The wider context

In this chapter we will focus on England, the largest of four countries of the United Kingdom (UK), with 84 per cent of the UK population. There are differ-ences across the four countries in areas of responsibility. For example, ECEC is a responsibility of the individual governments, while parental leave and subsidies for childcare, rest with the UK government as a whole.

Conditions for family life provide an important context for ECEC provision and the workforce. In the UK, just under 60 per cent of mothers of children under five years of age are in employment, although many work part-time. Up to 20 months of parental leave is available for mothers and fathers, but only six weeks is well paid and most women return to work before the end of unpaid entitle-ment. Take up of leave provision varies according to level of remuneration, type of employer and employment, so those who are self-employed, employed in the private sector or where the leave is unpaid or paid at a low rate are less likely to use leave provisions (Moss 2014). Moss (2014) points out that there is a 16-month gap between the end of parental leave provision and ECEC entitlement at the age of three; provision for children below the age of three and for longer hours above the age of three is paid for by parents' fees, although there are tax credits for lower-earning families.

Developing ECEC provision in England since the 1990s

Before 1997, ECEC provision in England was very patchy (OECD 2001). The split system of care and education provision for different purposes, run by different government and local authority departments, with staff who often had different professional backgrounds meant it was highly fragmented. Through the 1990s there was growing evidence of the necessity of attending to the quality of both care *and* education in services for young children (DES 1990). Overall, the central and enduring features of early childhood education and care provision in England, leading up to the reforms that have taken place since the mid-1990s were:

- A belief in mothers as the best carers for young children and parents as responsible for upbringing;
- A reliance on the private market, with subsidies for some forms of provision;
- Part-time provision of early education, for children aged three and four in schools and nursery schools, staffed by early childhood teachers and nursery nurses;
- Day nursery provision, full-time or part-time, for children of working parents who could afford the fees and for children with high levels of social or emotional need, where the occupational model was nursery nurse or childcare worker;
- Childminders or family day carers, in domestic premises, private but regulated and inspected;
- Playgroups, run by voluntary associations, low fees and low wages for staff, regulated and inspected;
- Changes in the local authority role for supporting and regulating services in the private and voluntary sector leading, eventually, to an inspection role for a national body.

(Office for Standards in Education / Ofsted)

From the mid-1990s, family life and ECEC became a party political issue. Real change came with the election of a Labour government in 1997. For the first time, ECEC became the target of widespread reform aimed at helping families combining work and care responsibilities and addressing the high level of child poverty in the UK. A National Childcare Strategy aimed to reduce fragmentation and to ensure good-quality, affordable childcare for children from birth to 14 in every neighbourhood, including both formal childcare and support for informal arrangements (DfEE 1998). A comprehensive reform of children's services in England within an ethos based on children's rights and positive outcomes for children, particularly for children at risk took place in 2003 (Her Majesty's Treasury [HMT] 2003). Following this, in 2004, a Ten Year Childcare Strategy emphasised the themes of 'choice and flexibility' for parents, 'quality' of provision, a skilled workforce with a 'strengthened qualification and career structure' and 'affordability'. Specific measures included a new programme called Sure Start, tax subsidies for childcare costs and increased entitlement to free early education. The Sure Start programme, based on the US Head Start programme, brought together care provision, early education and support for families into Children's Centres (Department for Education and Skills [DfES] 2006) for children up to four years of age. The ambition was to have a Sure Start children's centre in every neighbourhood.

In 2006, the OECD noted 'tremendous progress' in developing ECEC in England, mostly in relation to expansion of Children's Centres, and developing before- and after-school provision. Spending on children's services in the UK quadrupled between 1997–2007, from GBP 1.1 billion in 1996/7, to GBP 4.4 billion by 2007/8 (OECD 2006).

The aim to unite care and education was embodied in a new Department for Children, Schools and Families (DCSF) in 2006.[1] However, the integration of policy had limits. Responsibility for children's health remained with the Department of Health. At local authority level, new Directors of Children's Services, usually from an education background, integrated planning and delivery of services. But the two main occupational models of nursery nurse and teacher did not reflect these changes.

Since 2010, when a Conservative-led coalition came into government, with an 'austerity' agenda aimed at cutting publicly funded services, around 1,000 Children's Centres have closed or their remit has become more targeted on disadvantaged families. There has been a policy shift towards 'sector-led self-improvement', which means the workforce strategy relies on leaders and managers in services to develop and undertake training and professionalise the workforce. Other significant players, such as higher education, have a more marginal role in professional training (Taylor 2014).

ECEC provision

ECEC provision from birth to five year olds consists of a number of different types of care and education and play focused settings, run by organisations and employers – known as 'providers' – in the private, voluntary and independent (PVI) and public (maintained) sectors.[2] All provision is required to be registered and is regulated by Ofsted, including regular inspections. According to a regular government survey (Brind et al. 2014), major trends over the period 2008–2013 were:

- A steady increase in the number of full day care providers (year round, all day) to 17,900 in 2013 compared to 13,800 in 2008;
- A decrease in sessional (part-time) providers. In 2013 there were 7,100, down from 8,500 in 2008;

- A decrease in the number of childminders: 46,100 in 2013 from 56,100 in 2008;
- A decrease of around 10 per cent in the number of nursery schools (450 in 2008, down to 400 in 2013), and an increase in the number of primary schools with reception and nursery classes (up from 6,700 in 2008 to 7,600 in 2013).

In 2013, 61 per cent of full day care provision was in the private for profit sector, 30 per cent was run by voluntary organisations and nine per cent was in the public sector, mostly children's centres (Brind et al. 2014). By 2010 there were 3,500 designated Children's Centres in England. Children's Centres did not replace existing provision but extended it in areas of social deprivation; and only those located in the 30 per cent most deprived communities had to offer integrated early education and childcare places alongside support and advice services. In other areas providing ECEC places this was optional, although there were some activities for children on site. However, between 2010 and 2012, 401 Children's Centres closed, merged or reduced the universal service provision, focusing instead on the most disadvantaged families (Moss 2013). Despite these cutbacks, Children's Centres are popular, and 'more than one million households are now using Children's Centres every year... [which] equates to roughly 42 per cent of all households in England with at least one child aged 0-5 years', and that this includes 64 per cent of 'vulnerable' families (4Children 2013: 14).

In 2013 there were 2,204,400 childcare and early years places (combining full day care, sessional care, childminders, nursery schools, primary schools with nursery and reception classes and primary schools with no nursery classes (Brind et al. 2014). About 90 per cent of three and four year olds attended some form of early education provision, more than half in maintained part-time education places (Huskinson et al. 2014). Nearly 40 per cent of children under three were enrolled in services, many part-time (ibid.) This lower rate of participation for young children was due to a combination of part-time parental (mothers) employment, a preference for informal childcare by family members at this age and the high cost of childcare places for this age group.

The average cost of sending a child under two to nursery part-time (25 hours) is around £115 per week or £6,000 per year. A part-time place with a childminder costs about £100 per week (Rutter 2015). Among OECD countries, only Switzerland has more expensive childcare than the UK (Rogers 2012).

The ECEC curriculum

Since 2008 all providers of ECEC services have been required to work to a curricular framework called *The Early Years Foundation Stage* (EYFS), for children from birth to five (DCSF 2008). The EYFS set out 69 Early Learning Goals (ELGs) which most children were expected to reach by the end of the EYFS and these were explicitly linked to the competences set out for a new occupational role, the EYPs, who were intended to lead practice in the setting (see below). The EYFS goals were reduced to 17 in 2011, and grouped into three 'prime areas': personal, social and emotional development; communication and language; and physical development. These reforms were designed to make the EYFS less bureaucratic and more focused on young children's learning and development (Staggs 2012).

The ELG approach represents a 'schoolification' of early childhood because of strong links to the primary curriculum for children aged 5 to 11 years (OECD 2006: 62), and as encouraging practitioners to focus on strategic compliance with national requirements (Goouch 2010). In 2014, the EYFS was amended to strengthen safeguarding and welfare requirements and to set standards for the learning, development and care of children from birth to five years old. All provision – including preschools, nurseries, school reception classes and childminders – must follow the EYFS. Early learning focuses on three 'prime' and four 'specific' areas of learning. Prime areas are: communication and language, physical development and personal and social development. Specific areas of learning are: literacy, mathematics, understanding the world, expressive arts and design. Assessment of children's learning and development takes place through an observation based Early Years Foundation Stage Profile as a record of each child's learning and development (https:www.gov.uk/early-years-foundation-stage, accessed 11 February 2015).

Despite limited references to the importance of play, exploration and active learning, an increasing trend towards the 'schoolification' of ECEC services is reflected in the new standards for the EYT role, which state they 'promote teaching and learning to ensure children's "school readiness"...'. Further, EYTs are required to 'understand the continuum' of the early years curriculum through to primary school. References are made to setting high expectations, including goals that 'challenge' and 'stretch' children; promoting good progress and 'outcomes'; making accurate and 'productive' use of assessment; and modelling and implementing 'effective' education and care (NCTL 2013).

The ECEC workforce

Secondary analysis of the Labour Force Survey for England showed that, in 2012–2014, there were approximately 313,000 childcare workers (including nursery nurses, childminders and related occupations, and playworkers). Ninety-eight per cent of the childcare workers were female, and the mean age was 36 years. Twelve per cent of this group had a degree-level qualification and their pay was about ten per cent above the minimum wage. There were also 399,000 nursery and primary education teachers. It is not possible to tell how many of these teachers work only with children under five. Among the teachers, 15 per cent were male, and older, mostly between 35 and 49 years of age. Almost 90 per cent had a degree as their highest qualification and their pay was almost three times that of the childcare workers. There are also 320,000 educational assistants, whose role it is to assist teachers in nursery, primary and secondary classrooms (Owen 2015).

Within this general picture, there are approximately 13,300 practitioners who hold EYP Status (Taylor 2014). The development of the EYP model was perhaps the most significant of a series of attempts to professionalise and upskill the ECEC workforce at graduate level. It arose following a government-led consultation on the children's workforce, which accepted the need for a graduate professional in early years settings (DfES 2005). Two occupational models were proposed: a pedagogue, drawing on evidence from Europe, particularly Denmark, and a 'new teacher', with inspiration from New Zealand. Both these were rejected and the EYP model was 'produced out of thin air' (Moss 2008: 127).

The need for a graduate-led profession was based on the findings of influential research by Sylva et al. (2003; 2010), which linked the quality of ECEC provision with the quality of staff. The effect of high-quality staff was particularly marked for the social and learning gains of children living in economically disadvantaged areas. The most effective settings in the Sylva et al. study were those that combined care and education, were in the public sector and employed graduate-level trained teachers. In line with this, the government saw reforming the workforce through a programme of training and qualifications as crucial for raising the quality of services. Sylva et al. (2003; 2010) recommended there should be a good proportion of trained teachers, or *equivalent*, holding lead positions in ECEC settings in order to achieve good outcomes. Equivalence, however, was never defined, leading to lack of clarity in relation to status and pay, as discussed below.

The EYP model built on earlier attempts at professionalisation, which included the introduction of Early Childhood Studies degrees at Bachelor level and Early Years Foundation Degrees (FdAs) linked to a supervisory Senior Practitioner role in private and voluntary sector nurseries (this role was rendered obsolete in 2007/8). An FdA early years graduate could study further and achieve a Bachelor's degree and Qualified Teacher Status. There was no automatic link to improved pay and conditions of employment with these roles, which was a recurring theme in the implementation of the EYP model (and indeed the more recent EYT model), as discussed below. The experience of short-lived occupational models and lack of action following consultation with stakeholders left many in the sector, including students, practitioners, experienced managers and professional networks, feeling disenchanted with government (Miller 2008).

Introducing the EYP as a new graduate model faced a major upskilling problem: few childcare workers held a degree (Simon et al. 2006; DCSF 2007) and this was especially the case in the private and voluntary sectors. A way had to be found to address the gap between the quality of staff in PVI settings and those in the most effective public settings without disrupting the largely marketised approach to ECEC provision.

At the same time, there was a drive to bring coherence to the qualifications for the children's workforce as a whole. In 2006 a National Qualifications Framework was introduced with eight levels that matched academic and vocational qualifications. The levels were:

- Level 1: GCSE Grades D–G, Foundation level GNVQ, Level 1 NVQ
- Level 2: GCSE Grades A★–C; Level 2 diploma

- Level 3: A Levels; Level 3 Diploma in Child Care and Education
- Level 4: Certificate in Early Years Practice, Certificate of Higher Education
- Level 5 or Intermediate: BTEC Higher National Diploma, Foundation Degree in Early Years
- Level 6 or Honours: BA Early Childhood Studies Bachelor of Education (BEd), Early Years Professional Status, Early Years Teacher
- Level 7 or Masters, PGCE, National Professional Qualification for Integrated Centre Leadership (NPQICL)
- Level 8: Doctorate

There is still a lack of clarity about the equivalence of EYPs to Qualified Teachers. As the above makes clear, EYP sits at the same level as Bachelor degree (Level 6) and is deemed equivalent to Qualified Teacher Status (QTS), yet most teachers have a PGCE, which sits at Level 7 on the framework and usually carried Masters' credits.

EYP Status

The occupational role of EYP was designed to lead practice in Children's Centres and in PVI settings. There were four routes to gaining EYP Status. These were:

- A three months part-time validation pathway (for experienced candidates in order to 'validate' existing knowledge, skills and experience);
- A six month part-time extended professional development pathway (short EPD) (for experienced candidates to 'top up' their knowledge across the full age range from birth to 5 years);
- A 15 month part-time extended professional development pathway (long EPD) so that candidates with an existing Level 5 qualification could 'top up' their knowledge;
- A full-time 12 month training pathway (for candidates with a Bachelor degree in an unrelated subject and limited experience of children from birth to five).

(CWDC 2006)

The main remit of the EYP role was to lead practice and be a change agent for other workers in the setting. It was also designed to be a holistic model and overcome the historic split between care for the youngest children (from birth to three years) and more 'education' focused practice with older age groups of children (three to five years). The training was run as a collaboration between training providers, including universities, and employers. The implementation of the EYP model was part of a wider investment in ECEC. Mathers et al. (2012: 12) described the background:

> Funding to support workforce reform in the PVI sector was provided by the Transformation Fund (TF), [...which provided] £250 million in funding to

early years settings via their local authorities. In April 2008 the TF was super-seded by the Graduate Leader Fund (GLF), which provided a further £305 million in ring-fenced funding to support all full day care PVI sector provid-ers in employing a graduate or Early Years Professional (EYP) by 2015. The ring-fenced GLF funding ended in March 2011; from April 2011 LAs [were] required to support the development of EYPs in PVI settings through the Early Intervention Grant.

The purpose of the graduate leader fund was to allow local authorities (LAs) to design their own workforce development systems, which would take into account local contexts and meet the policy goal of employing at least one EYP in every PVI setting by 2015 and, in the most disadvantaged areas, could support two graduate professional leaders per setting. Each LA was expected to set its own targets for local workforce development. Outcomes were then measured against the baseline of the number of graduates leading practice in PVI full day care settings in each area (Mathers et al. 2012).

Overall, the EYP role brought significant gains to children's care and education, particularly those in the age range 30 months to five years. Mathers et al. (2012: 6) drew attention to improvements in a 'number of individual dimensions of practice, including: positive staff-child interactions; support for communication, language and literacy; reasoning/thinking skills and scientific understanding; provision of a developmentally appropriate schedule; and providing for individual needs and diversity'. The EYP was also often a catalyst for improvements in settings, in both child-led learning and more structural changes, such as use of key worker sys-tems, parent-practitioner relationships and parental involvement with the setting. However, the same study found that there was little evidence that EYPs improved the quality of provision for younger children (from birth to 30 months) (Mathers et al. 2012).

Raising the confidence of practitioners

A government-commissioned longitudinal evaluation of the impact of the EYP programme on the quality of their settings and their leadership roles found that EYPs were 'extremely positive' (Hadfield et al. 2012: 34) about gaining EYP Status. In this study of 41 EYPs employed in 30 settings drawn from the private, voluntary and maintained sector, including two family day care providers, over 90 per cent of the respondents said acquiring the EYP Status had increased their confi-dence as a practitioner and had helped them to develop their knowledge and skills. Study respondents drew attention to the benefits of theoretical knowledge and its relationship to practice, and led, in the words of one respondent, an experienced Children's Centre Leader working with under twos, to gaining 'respect for my skills and abilities, which has allowed me to support my staff effectively' (Hadfield et al. 2012: 31). Similarly, Roberts-Holmes' (2013) analysis of focus group discus-sions with 26 EYPs in one local authority, again drawn from a range of types of

ECEC setting, found that the process of becoming an EYP had given practitioners newfound confidence to lead change. One, again highly experienced, said 'my role as EYP gives me personal autonomy and authority to lead my staff, communicate with parents and engage with the children at a very professional and personal level' (Roberts-Holmes 2013: 345). A better understanding of the relationship of theory to practice was also mentioned as a benefit of the EYP training in two focus groups carried out by Miller and Cameron (2010).

However, staff who were already qualified as teachers felt the EYP training confirmed what they already knew and represented 'jumping through more hoops' (Roberts-Holmes 2013: 345). One persistent problem with the EYP, as a new role, was that it was not well understood, either by parents, the public at large, or within the field (Miller and Cameron 2010; Hadfield et al. 2012). This may have been overcome with time, but meant that the newfound confidence of practitioners was challenged at the level of everyday interaction with users of the services.

Leadership and the change agent role

One of the intentions of the EYP was that practitioners would be equipped to lead practice in the workplace and inspire other practitioners around them (CWDC 2010, cited in McDowell Clark 2012). Leadership within ECEC had become a live issue, with, for example, specific leadership programmes available, such as the National Professional Qualification in Integrated Centre Leadership (NPQICL) (Whalley 2011). However, the EYP role was aimed at *within setting* leadership, and specifically at modelling good practice in order to address the quality of care and education in line with the findings of the Sylva et al. (2003) study. Early studies indicated that the 'change agent' role was proving difficult (Simpson 2010), particularly for those not already in senior positions (Miller and Cameron 2010). However, the Hadfield et al. (2012: 35) study found that 'over 80 per cent of EYPs overall felt that gaining EYPS had improved their ability to carry out improvements in their settings' and a similar proportion thought their status had improved. Importantly, the proportion of EYPs who thought their colleagues were receptive to their ideas rose between two phases of enquiry, from 49 per cent to 67 per cent (Hadfield et al. 2012).

McDowell Clark's (2012) study of the views of 28 graduates working as EYPs in a range of ECEC settings raised some complexities about the leadership role of EYPs. His respondents lacked confidence in their own leadership and were very aware of the limitations of their role as leaders from within practice. They had no mandate to impose change, particularly where they were not managers. They worked alongside less well-qualified practitioners who, they perceived, might feel inadequate or undervalued if confronted with their practice. Respondents discussed their changed role as a process of reviewing, adapting and reflecting on practice, having the confidence to make a change, often expressed as 'small steps', and, moreover, coming to believe in themselves as leaders. McDowell Clark (2012) concluded that EYPs could be seen as exercising 'catalytic leadership', wielding influence but not authority.

The characteristics of leadership in ECEC settings have been noted in previous research. Effective settings are those where the leadership qualities of contextual literacy and commitment to collaboration and to the improvement of children's learning were strongly represented (Siraj-Blatchford and Manni 2007). Contextual literacy is the ability of EYPs to read the dynamics of their particular setting and decide how best to respond in their practice leadership role. This finding resonates with Dalli et al.'s (2012) reference to 'a critical ecology of the profession,' which discusses a questioning approach to how professionals might act in different geographical, physical and cultural contexts. Leadership from within practice requires careful consideration. Significantly, it requires EYPs to be free from financial, administrative and managerial demands (Roberts-Holmes 2012) in order to focus on pedagogical leadership, as is the case for teachers employed in the maintained sector nursery schools and classes (Aubrey 2007).

Pay and conditions

Although EYPs were given equivalent status to early childhood teachers, their pay and conditions were left untouched (apart from some support to salaries through the GLF), meaning that, in effect, the role came with little improvement in pay and conditions. The maintained sector, historically, paid ECEC workers better than the PVI sector (Simon et al. 2006) and this has continued. Early on, a survey of EYPs revealed that they were concerned about future career prospects, professional development and pay and conditions (ASPECT 2009). Pay in the PVI sector is closely linked to the ability of parents to pay fees; despite some subsidy from tax credits, parents in England, as already noted, spend more of their net income on ECEC costs than in other OECD countries so there was limited room for improvement in salaries. Brind et al. (2014) found that graduates in full day care settings (mostly in the PVI sector) earned £8.70 per hour, on average, and £12 per hour if employed in Children's Centres (mostly in the maintained sector). Working as a graduate in the PVI ECEC sector meant earning little more than half the national (graduate and nongraduate) mean hourly wage for the UK (£15.19 per hour) (Brind et al. 2014). The EYP model threatened to 'ghettoise' EYPs in the lower paid private and voluntary sector (Hevey 2007).

There was also an issue of parity with teachers. The EYP Status was deemed to be equivalent to Qualified Teacher Status (QTS). However, this did not work out in practice. Firstly, in relation to the status of the two roles, the standards for both teachers and EYPs were set at Level 6 on the National Qualifications Framework, suggesting equivalence. The workforce council (CWDC) advised that practitioners with QTS should consider the need for additional training and recommended that qualified teachers without training in child development from birth to five should undertake EYPS. Devereux and Cable (2008) drew attention to the differences between QTS and EYPS standards, arguing that QTS standards make scant reference to the needs of young children. Despite rhetoric around equivalent status for the two roles, in reality, qualified teachers in the main lead on the EYFS in maintained settings (i.e. nursery schools and schools), whilst EYPs are restricted to the PVI sector. This lack of parity of EYPS in relation to qualified teachers and the lack of national guidance on commensurate levels of pay meant that the position of EYPs in relation to qualified teachers remained ambiguous. With prescience, Hevey (2007) questioned the long-term affordability of EYPs once initial government funding through the GLF ended, as indeed they were replaced by the new role of EYT in 2013.

What has been learned?

A longstanding problem for the ECEC sector has been an absence of clear, long-term thinking about the purpose and role of early childhood services, leading to the growth of occupational titles, forms of training and types of provision (Abbott and Pugh 1998). Shifts towards professionalisation, of which the EYP model is one, have not yet dented the diversity of the workforce (Miller and Cable 2008). Workforce reform has happened in a piecemeal way, hampered by the absence of a strong collective voice and delaying the development of a single professional role and a coherent policy (Abbott and Pugh 1998; Miller and Cable 2008).

A major problem with the EYP initiative is that it did not address the need for more appropriately trained teachers in the ECEC sector. There are now more graduates working within the PVI sector, but they have not had the depth of training in pedagogical leadership that early childhood teachers have had. Critically, the EYPs did not have the professional recognition, status and pay of teachers, so were not considered commensurate or equivalent occupations. A question was raised as to whether inserting 'professional' in the title meant other workers were less 'professional'? Perhaps, as Moss (2008) argues, it might be better to recognise 'core workers' in the field as professionals as well as leaders. Fenech and Sumsion (2007: 119) warn of the 'othering' of those deemed not to be 'professional'.

However, the EYP did, as with earlier attempts at professionalisation, stimulate a great appetite for learning while in practice, or continuous professional development. The initiative drew the 'line in the sand' that established the principle that caring for and educating very young children requires a higher level of qualification than was accepted hitherto. That it was a national programme undoubtedly helped, but the most significant factors in successful implementation appeared to be structural, in the form of financial resources in the GLF, local authority support to build an infrastructure for peer learning for EYPs, as well as locating training within university-based educational provision.

Since the advent of the Coalition government in 2010, as noted above, the EYP role has been replaced by the EYT with revised standards. The Nutbrown Review of qualifications (2012: 6–8) expressed concern that existing qualifications did not always prepare practitioners with 'the knowledge, skills and understanding they need to give babies and young children high quality experiences' and set out a new long-term vision based on raising standards of education required to be employed in the sector, including English and maths. Further, noting the problems with the lack of parity with teachers, the review recommended establishing a specialist route to QTS, so as to 'raise the status of the sector, increase professionalism and improve quality'. Taylor (2014: 7) confirmed that entrants to the EYT training programme will be required to pass English and maths skills tests 'making it the same as for primary teacher training'. Whereas the EYP role was firmly pitched in the 'holistic' care and education domain, the current direction of travel is now towards 'schoolification', with considerable emphasis placed on early literacy and numeracy, claiming that 'parents trust nurseries to help their children learn to speak and to add up' and that 'a more skilled workforce will increase the quality of support for children … and will ensure they are ready to learn and thrive at school' (Taylor 2014: 8–9).

Conclusions

The EYP was one example among many of attempts to address the competence requirements for early childhood education and care practice in a marketised and conceptually split system. A gradual recognition, supported by research and scholarship, of the importance of the early childhood phase, led to various attempts at higher education level qualifications. There were, in addition, many and varied qualifications available for ECEC workers at lower levels, which were also under scrutiny and reform during the period in question. Notions of competence for early childhood practitioners and leaders have had to incorporate a widening agenda to do with children and their families, family support, employability of parents, protection of 'vulnerable' children, children with disabilities, working with professionals from other agencies and backgrounds, and a new, national foundation stage, curriculum. At the same time there was a substantial policy push towards integration of care and education, both at administrative levels and funding levels. PVI childcare settings, for example, were required to have access to teacher input, something that was always in place in the maintained sector, of which nursery schools represented the 'gold standard'.

Pragmatic and piecemeal responses to try to raise the profile and shift the level of competence and recognition, although often welcomed in the field, have not fundamentally addressed the paucity of public investment in provision. A continued reliance on the PVI sector, and parents' fees, to supply high-quality provision, means the pay, status and professional recognition of the workforce is under pressure. The EYP model, and those that take its place without attending to pay and conditions, are often notable for hasty consultations and attempts to achieve a graduate workforce 'on the cheap'. There is now research evidence, through the EYP experience, about the intricacies of leading practice from within. There is an outstanding question about whether the useful lessons of separating pedagogical leadership from managerial and administrative leadership have been incorporated into the new EYT model, to identify whether and how it contributes to effective learning and caring for young children of all ages, and in socially advantaged as well as disadvantaged areas.

Notes

1 Over the period in question the government department for education changed its name several times, from the Department for Education and Employment, to the Department of Education and Skills, to the Department for Children, Schools and Families, to, in 2010, the Department of Education.
2 The government also counts after-school clubs and holiday clubs as part of its childcare and early years provision, but this has been omitted here for the sake of clarity.

References

Abbot, L. and Pugh, G. (1998) *Training to Work in the Early Years*. Buckingham: The Open University Press.
ASPECT EYP Survey (2009) In their own words: EYPs speak out. http://www.aspect.org.uk/eyp/wp-content/uploads/2009/04/eyp-p-survey-report.pdf, accessed 23 February 2015.
Aubrey, C. (2007) *Leading and Managing in the Early Years*. London: Sage.
Brind, R., McGinigal, S., Lewis, J. and Ghezelayagh, S. (TNS BMRB), with Ransom, H., Robson, J., Street, C. and Renton, Z. (NCB Research Centre) (2014) *Childcare and Early Years Providers Survey 2013* TNS BMRB Report JN 117328 September 2014.
Cameron, C. (2011) Competence – what do you need to know and do? *Children in Europe*, 21, September.
Children's Workforce Development Council (CWDC) (2006) *Early Years Professional Prospectus*. Leeds: CWDC.
Dalli, C., Miller, L. and Urban, M. (2012) Early childhood grows up towards a critical ecology of the profession, in Dalli, C., Miller, L. and Urban, M. (Eds.) *Early Childhood Grows Up Towards a Critical Ecology of the Profession*. Heidelberg, London, New York: Springer, pp. 3–21.
Department for Children, Schools and Families (DCSF) (2008) *Statutory Framework for the Early Years Foundation Stage*. Nottingham: DCSF Publications.
Department for Education and Employment (DfEE) (1998) *Meeting the Childcare Challenge: A Framework and Consultation Document*. London: HMSO.
Department for Education and Science (DES) (1990) *Starting with Quality*. London: HMSO.
Department for Education and Skills (DfES) (2005) *Common Core of Skills and Knowledge for the Children's Workforce*. Nottingham: DfES Publications.
Department for Education and Skills (DfES) (2006) Departmental Report. https://www.gov.uk/government/uploads/system/uploads/attachment_data/file/324573/DFE_Departmental_Report_2006.pdf, accessed 21 December 2015.
Devereux, J. and Cable, C. (2008) The early years teacher, in Miller, L. and Cable, C. (Eds.) *Professionalism in the Early Years*. London: Hodder Education, pp. 41–54.
Early Years Foundation Stage Profile (2015) https:www.gov.uk/early-years-foundation-stage, accessed 11 February 2015.
Fenech, M. and Sumsion, J. (2007) Early childhood teachers and regulation: complicating power relations using a Foucauldian lens, *Contemporary Issues in Early Childhood*, 8 (2) 109–122.
4Children (2013) Children's Centres Census 2013: a national overview of developments in children's centres. http://www.4children.org.uk/Files/8dd559e9-acc8-4030-a787-a28800f72e3d/Children_Centre_Census_2013_FINAL_AM.pdf, accessed 27 February 2015.
Goouch, K. (2010) *Towards Excellence in Early Years Education: Exploring Narratives of Experience*. Abingdon: Routledge.
Hadfield, M., Jopling, M., Needham, M., Waller, T., Coleyshaw, L., Mahmoud, E. and Royle, R. (2012) *Longitudinal Study of Early Years Professional Status: An Exploration of*

Progress, Leadership and Impact. https://www.gov.uk/government/uploads/system/uploads/attachment_data/file/183418/DfE-RR239c_report.pdf, accessed 21/12/2015.

Her Majesty's Treasury (2003) *Every Child Matters* (Cm 5860). London: TSO.

Hevey, D. (2007) Early Years Professional Status: an Initiative in Search of a Strategy. Prague: 17th EECERA Conference, 30 August 2007.

House of Commons Children, Schools and Families Committee (2009–2010) *Sure Start Children's Centres, Fifth Report of Session 2009–10*, HC 130-1 http://www.publications.parliament.uk/pa/cm200910/cmselect/cmchilsch/130/130i.pdf, accessed 21/12/2015.

Huskinson, T., Kostadintcheva, K., Greevy, H., Salmon, C., Dobie, S., Medien, K. with Gilby, N., Littlewood, M. and D'Souza, J. (2014) *Childcare and Early Years Survey of Parents 2012–2013*, SFR06/2014, available from https://www.gov.uk/government/uploads/system/uploads/attachment_data/file/275992/SFR06-2014_Childcare_and_Early_Years_Survey_of_Parents_2012-13_final.pdf, accessed 27 February 2015.

Mackenzie, P., Mitchell, P. and Oliver, P. (Eds.) (1995) *Competence and Accountability in Education*. Aldershot: Arena

Mathers, S., Ranns, H., Karemaker, A., Moody, A., Sylva, K., Graham, J. and Siraj-Blatchford, I. (2012) *Evaluation of the Graduate Leader Fund, Final report Research Report* DFE-RR144 2012.

McDowell Clark, R. (2012) 'I've never thought of myself as a leader but ...' The early years professional and catalytic leadership, *EECERJ*, 20, 3, 391–401.

McGillivray, G. (2010) Constructions of professional identity, in Miller, L. and Cable, C. (Eds.) *Professionalization, Leadership and Management in the Early Years*. London: SAGE.

Miller, L. (2008) Developing new professional roles in the early years, in Miller, L. and Cable, C. (Eds.) *Professionalism in the Early Years*. London: Hodder Education.

Miller, L. and Cable, C. (Eds.) (2008) *Professionalism in the Early Years*. London: Hodder Education.

Miller, L. and Cameron, C. (2010) *The Integrated Qualifications Framework and the Early Years Professional Status: A Shift Towards a Graduate Led Workforce*. Unpublished report for University of East London/University of Ghent.

Moss, P. (2008) The democratic and reflective professional: rethinking and reforming the early years workforce, in Miller, L. and Cable, C. (Eds.) *Professionalism in the Early Years*, London: Hodder Education.

Moss, P. (2013) *Early Childhood Education and Care: a Case Study of England 1997–2013*. Thomas Coram Research Unit Institute of Education University of London, unpublished study.

Moss, P. (Ed.) (2014) *10th International Review of Leave Policies and Related Research 2014*, Thomas Coram Research Unit Institute of Education University of London, available at: http://www.leavenetwork.org/fileadmin/Leavenetwork/Annual_reviews/2014_annual_review_korr.pdf, accessed 27/2/2015.

National College for Teaching and Leadership (NCTL) (2013) *Early Years Teachers' Standards*, available from https://www.gov.uk/government/publications/early-years-teachers-standards.

National Foundation for Educational Research (NFER)/Children's Workforce Development Council (CWDC) (2009) *Evaluation of the Career Developments of Early Years Professional (EYPs) Key Findings*. http://www.cwdcouncil.org.uk/assets/0000/5565/EYP_Evaluation_Summary_Report_June09.pdf accessed 15/7/2010.

National Qualifications Framework (2014) *The Framework for Higher Education Qualifications. Part A. Setting and maintaining Academic Standards. The Framework for Higher Education Qualifications of UK Degree Awarding Bodies*. October 2014. http://www.qaa.ac.uk/en/Publications/Documents/qualifications-frameworks.pdf, accessed 21 December 2015.

Nutbrown, C (2012) *Foundations for Quality: The Independent Review of Early Education and Childcare Qualifications. Final Report*. https://www.gov.uk/government/uploads/system/uploads/attachment_data/file/175463/Nutbrown-Review.pdf, accessed 12 February 2015.

Oberhümer, P. (2000) Conceptualizing the professional role in early childhood centers: emerging profiles in four European countries, Early Childhood Research and Practice, 2, 2, http://ecrp.uiuc.edu/v2n2/oberhuemer.html, accessed 21 December 2015.

OECD (2001) *Starting Strong I: Early Childhood Education and Care*. Paris: OECD Publishing.

OECD (2005) The Definition and Selection of Competencies: Executive Summary, available at http://www.oecd.org/dataoecd/47/61/35070367.pdf, accessed 21 December 2015.

OECD (2006) *Starting Strong II: Early Childhood Education and Care*. Paris: OECD Publishing.

OECD (2010) Family Database, available at http://www.oecd.org/dataoecd/46/13/3786 4698.pdf, accessed 21 December 2015.

Owen, C. (2015) Personal communication.

Roberts-Holmes, G. (2013) The English early years professional status (EYPS) and the 'split' early childhood education and care (ECEC) system, *EECERJ*, 21, 3, 339–352.

Rogers, S. (2012) *Child Care Costs: How the UK Compares with the World,* available at http://www.theguardian.com/news/datablog/2012/may/21/child-care-costs-compared-britain, accessed 9 March 2015.

Rutter, J. (2015) Childcare Costs Survey, available at http://www.familyandchildcaretrust.org/childcare-costs-surveys, accessed 9 March 2015.

Simon, A., Owen, C., Moss, P., Petrie, P., Cameron, C., Potts, P. and Wigfall, V. (2006) *Working Together* Volume 1: *Secondary Analysis of the Labour Force Survey to Map the Numbers and Characteristics of the Occupations Working within Social Care, Childcare, Nursing and Education*, London: Thomas Coram Research, Institute of Education, University of London, available at http://eprints.ioe.ac.uk/4132/1/Simon2008WorkingTogether.pdf, accessed 27 February 2015.

Simpson, D. (2010) Being professional? Conceptualising early years professionalism in England, *EECERJ*, 18, 1, 5–14.

Siraj-Blatchford, I. and Manni, L. (2007) *Effective Leadership in the Early Years Sector: The ELEYS study*. London: Institute of Education University of London.

Staggs, L. (2012) The rhetoric and reality of a national strategy for early education and assessment, in Miller, L. and Hevey, D. (Eds.) *Policy Issues in the Early Years*. London: SAGE.

Sylva, K., Melhuish, E., Sammons, P., Siraj-Blatchford, I., Taggart, B. and Elliot, K. (2003) *The Effective Provision of Pre-School Education (EPPE) Project: Findings from the Pre-School Period – Summary of Findings*. London: Institute of Education and Sure Start.

Sylva, K., Melhuish, E., Sammons, P., Siraj-Blatchford, I. and Taggart, B. (2010) *Early Childhood Matters: Evidence from the Effective Preschool and Primary Education Project*. London: Routledge.

Taylor, C. (2014) Transforming the early years workforce: leadership and improvement aspirations for the early years workforce of the future the journey to get there and how to make early years a career of choice. Speech given at National Day Nurseries Association Conference, 19 June.

Urban, M., Lazzari, A., Vandenbroeck, M., Peeters, J. and Van Laere, K. (2011) *Competence Requirements for Early Childhood Education and Care*. London and Ghent: UEL and UGent.

Whalley, M.E. (2011) Leading and Managing in the Early Years: Towards a New Understanding, in Miller, L. and Cable, C. (Eds.) *Professionalization, Leadership and Management in the Early Years*. London: Sage.

8

FROM RESEARCH TO POLICY

The case of early childhood and care

Nóra Milotay

Introduction

While research seeks to show the complexity of issues in a nuanced way, policy looks for quick and efficient solutions supported by scientific evidence. Policy makers often feel that researchers cannot provide them with the exact evidence they need and researchers think that policy makers oversimplify the issues. While research and policy both wish to contribute to the ultimate aim of improving people's lives, they approach it in very different ways. The efficient communication of research and policy is, however, indispensable both for the development of meaningful policies and for the formulation of meaningful research questions. It is clearly a challenge to create a policy or strategy that is concise and that can truly push the agenda forward, and which researchers and practitioners and politicians alike would like to see implemented.

What matters for a policy agenda to go forward? What are the main ingredients for making an agenda stronger in the European policy arena? Important ingredients certainly include: the existence of policy relevant evidence (research[1] and knowledge[2] from the field), a willingness and room in policy making to take this up, well-functioning governance[3], allowing for good communication channels between the two worlds, and strong stakeholder support. In addition policy making/policy formation is not a linear, logical or rational process (Fazekas and Burns, 2012, pp. 7–8). Finally the particularity of European policy making is that it responds to very diverse geographical, socio-economic, political and cultural spaces, which pull it apart.

In this broader context this chapter tells two stories: the first concerns the process of European policy making – the refined back and forth between knowledge, research, expertise (including practice) and policy; the second the (re)rise of early childhood education and care (ECEC) on the European policy agenda. The two are of course related and beyond conscious decisions taken, conjunctures of random circumstances also matter a great deal. It is also important that the story is told by a European policy maker. The two parallel stories should show the dialogue between research and policy in the particular field of ECEC and also the potential to contribute to counterbalance the current tendency to draw exclusively upon evidence that is quantifiable and measurable at the expense of cultural, social contexts and sector specificity.

How ECEC appeared on the education agenda in 2011

Education is a soft policy area, very much guided by the principle of subsidiarity at European level. There is no binding legislation, and only a few tools are available to genuinely influence policies in the Member States: programmes like Erasmus+ and Horizon 2020; political cooperation such as under the Europe 2020 Strategy (including the European Semester[4]), and the Education and Training 2020 Strategy; and finally the Open Method of Coordination. The Europe 2020 Strategy covers all policy sectors, two out of the five headline targets concern education, early school leaving and tertiary graduates. The ET 2020 strategy deals exclusively with education and training and identifies four main priority areas of intervention: quality and efficiency, lifelong learning and mobility, equity and citizenship, and finally innovation and creativity. Within these four strategic areas it defines indicators and targets in order to emphasise the most important fields of intervention. The main targets are: participation in ECEC, low achievement in basic skills, employment rates of recent graduates and adult participation in lifelong learning. The Open Method of Coordination allows Member States (through their representatives) to participate in peer-learning and peer-review and to define common objectives, develop reference tools, including indicators and benchmarks for policy development and monitoring. There is therefore only guidance at European level.

Due to the soft nature of education policy at European level there are many forces and players at different levels pushing and pulling before a consensus is forged that is accepted at political level. The steering of this process and the educational systems to which they apply are both complex. The challenging questions are: how is knowledge generated and then used for policy making? What really influences the decisions so as to push for certain policies? What role is the EU playing in this complex set-up? Ideally the EU can frame a theoretically impartial discussion across national contexts and thus distil the elements of an ideal policy, of a vision of the ultimate best practice. But policy practice is never that straightforward.

In the case of ECEC there can be many rationales behind a given policy agenda at European level. ECEC has become an important area for European policy cooperation in the last two decades. More recently and particularly against the escalation of the global crisis and the introduction of austerity measures, policies on the early years are on the agenda and are the subject of national policy debates in many countries, as they not only concern young children's education but also involve core questions around poverty, child protection, family policy, etc.

Different policy issues relating to ECEC have been identified during the last two decades, ranging mainly from issues of access (so as to help parents, mainly women, to (re)integrate into the labour market) to issues of the quality of ECEC provision, which focus more on the child, its family and their well-being. There are also many rationales behind the different policies, ranging from economic to cultural and social issues, such as the ideas that ECEC is particularly beneficial for disadvantaged groups, or that working mothers contribute to tax revenues (NESSE, 2009). Different rationales have held sway at different times and in different contexts. Currently, the economic arguments seem to dominate international (including European) debates but there is also a fast-growing tendency to focus more on social rationales. Most recently, the understanding of the importance of early years for later education and the increasing awareness of the importance of social and emotional skills for life and learning, including the idea of their malleability, have increasingly exposed and integrated ECEC into the education discourse. Finally, there is also a rough consensus about the usefulness and value of early intervention (Gromley, 2011).

Why is it then that accessible high-quality ECEC programmes have still not taken root?

A key obstacle that all ECEC programmes face is the absence of a politically powerful constituency. Children cannot vote, nor lobby, nor donate to political campaigns. So despite the consensus on its usefulness and valuable contribution to child development ECEC has not taken root, certainly not from a child's or child's rights perspective.

The issue of early years at European level was first raised in the context of increasing the number of childcare places. The main rationale behind European level policy considerations was to promote female labour market participation and to reconcile work and family life. The areas addressed were: the quality of services, parental leave, workplace measures and the sharing of responsibilities. In 1992 the European Council adopted a Recommendation (Council Recommendation, 1992) highlighting the importance of developing affordable, accessible and quality childcare services, while at the same time encouraging flexibility and diversity in these services in order to meet the needs and preferences of parents and their children.

The 1992 Recommendation was followed by *Quality Targets in Services for Young Children*, published by the European Commission Childcare Network in 1996. The Network was an expert group drawn from all Member States, established and supported by the European Commission. It started from the principles set out in the Council Recommendation, and framed 40 targets it argued were achievable by all Member States within a ten-year period. The targets were organised into nine areas: policy; finance; levels and types of services; education; staff–child ratios; staff employment and training; environment and health; parents and community; and performance. The document stressed that the targets were interdependent.

This document, however, did not have the status of an official document of the European Commission and thus has not been systematically followed up at European level.

Nevertheless, the access issue became more prominent on the European agenda. The 'Barcelona objectives' adopted by the Council of Ministers in 2002 (European Parliament, 2002) were essentially concerned with promoting access to employment and enabling parents, particularly women, to remain in employment, thus supporting gender equality. They promoted that: 33% of children from birth to three years and 90% of three to six year olds should be provided with full-day formal childcare[5] places by 2010. The European Council reiterated this commitment in the 2006 European Pact for Gender Equality and in the Roadmap for Equality between Women and Men (2006–2010), the Commission undertook to 'support the achievement of the Barcelona targets on childcare facilities'. The Structural Funds have also provided co-financing for measures to facilitate the reconciling of work with family life, including the construction of childcare facilities, the training of personnel and the provision of childcare services for parents seeking employment.

These initiatives reinforced the discourse on the quantitative aspects of ECEC mainly from a labour market perspective.

The Barcelona objectives played an important role in drawing the attention of national policy makers to the importance of early years services. The follow-up reports gave accurate mappings of the state-of-play in different countries in 2008 and 2012 (European Commission, 2008; European Commission, 2013a).

Besides the Barcelona targets, the European benchmark on ECEC participation, adopted by Member States as part of the Education and Training 2020 strategy, also offered Member States guidance on creating more childcare places from 2009 onwards.[6] It is not a target as such, it only suggested that at least 95% of children between four years old and the age of starting compulsory primary education should participate in early childhood education across the EU by 2020. In 2012 the early childhood education participation rate was 93.9%. Although there has been a general increase in the EU average rate of participation, a number of countries are far below the benchmark. In other countries rates are already above 95% (European Commission, 2014a).

After 2000 there were increasing requests from Member States to also address, at the European level, the issue of the quality of ECEC provision. In 2006, Ministers stated that ECEC can bring the highest rates of return over the lifelong learning cycle, especially for disadvantaged groups (Council Conclusions, 2006). In 2008 they agreed a series of priorities for cooperation at EU level on school policy issues, including how to ensure accessible, high-quality pre-school provision (Council Conclusions, 2008), and in 2009 they adopted a strategic framework for cooperation in education and training until 2020, which included among the priorities for the period 2009–2011 'to promote generalised equitable access and reinforce the quality of the provision and teacher support in pre-primary education' (Council Conclusions, 2009).

The Communication of the Commission on 'Early Childhood Education and Care: providing all our children with the best start for the world of tomorrow', adopted in 2011, responded to that request. To complement earlier considerations about work–life balance it put the child, his/her personal development and their families' well-being at the heart of policy considerations. It was the first time that ECEC was addressed not as a vehicle for the improvement of other policy fields but as an area of policy cooperation in itself, an area in its own right that has a big impact on children's present and future life trajectories. The Communication set out the key issues for future co-operation with the aim of improving access and quality of services from birth to the start of compulsory schooling. It called for universally accessible, well-integrated services that build on a joint vision of ECEC, for the most effective curricular frameworks and for the staff competences and governance arrangements necessary to deliver it. It emphasised the importance of a holistic approach to the children, thus a balanced approach to all their needs, physical, emotional, social and cognitive. The messages were based on the most up-to-date comparative research and discussions with well-known experts and international organisations, such as OECD, UNESCO, etc.

The follow-up Council Conclusions endorsed these plans and launched a process of policy co-operation at the European level on ECEC. They invited Member States to analyse their current situation as regards ECEC provision, with particular attention to accessibility and quality, and to reinforce measures to ensure equitable and generalised access to high-quality ECEC services, as well as to invest in ECEC as a growth enhancing measure. The Council also invited the Commission to support the exchange of good practice, to broaden the evidence base on ECEC and to monitor and report on progress towards the EU benchmark within the Open Method of Coordination. Thus at the European level a political commitment to address ECEC from the perspective of the child and their families was created with these documents.

Building a consensus in Europe about what constitutes quality in ECEC?

The main follow-up of these developments was the creation of a thematic working group of 25 Member State (plus Norway and Turkey) experts. Between 2012–2014 the Working Group's members – from a range of relevant sectors including education, social and family affairs – have worked together using the peer-learning methodology, i.e. Member States' experts have exchanged and synthesised their policy experiences, analysed and compared policy options, drawn on research about successful policies and made recommendations for good policy practice. The focus has been to review key policy actions, which have led to improvements in ECEC quality within the five key areas for quality identified by the group: access; workforce; the content of the curriculum offered to children; evaluation and monitoring; and governance and funding. The group has reviewed the existing evidence from policy and practice in Member States, as well as cross-national research findings and visited four different Member States, and investigated and analysed ECEC policy and practice there: Romania (access), Hungary (curriculum), Ireland (evaluation and monitoring) and Denmark (workforce). All group members have also collected relevant data on each subtheme in the context of their own country's experiences. The group distilled from this range of policies, research and practice the key issues for quality within these five broad areas. All of this led to the design of a proposal for a Quality Framework in ECEC, which was published in the final report of the group in the autumn of 2014.

The parallel stakeholder group had members from 55 European stakeholder organisations – such as International Step by Step Association, Eurochild, Platform of International Cooperation on Undocumented Migrants, but also UNESCO, World Bank and private foundations – which focused on questions of ECEC, as well as early school leaving (ESL). Due to the parallel on-going dialogue and consensus building with the stakeholder group, the final output (the framework proposal) is a product that is broadly supported. The experts of the working group and the stakeholder group tested and legitimised the relevant knowledge of the ECEC policy field and turned it into policy.

The quality framework proposal on ECEC forged a consensus about what constitutes high quality ECEC across Europe and what should be done to help improve practice on the ground.

The consensus and proposal was presented as a framework in order to embrace the diversity of ECEC systems, cultures, economies and politics in Europe. The issue of quality is uncharted territory and a very flexible concept open to a range of interpretations (Ozga et al., 2011). At the same time, in policy making it needs to be defined as something that is telling and triggers reflection on real policy challenges. As such it needs to be sector-specific too. ECEC is a young field in the European education policy discourse and it is a great challenge to integrate it into its mainstream while respecting its sector-specificity: the existence of a large number of informal and non-formal services, the very strong emphasis of care beside the education component, its justifiable reluctance to resemble the school system in many ways, including the concept of working towards pre-defined individual child outcomes. Linking research policy and practice in meaningful ways, the Working Group and the stakeholder group did help to reconnect the ECEC discourse with current public debates about the democratic establishment too. The end-product (the framework proposal) is an open, flexible tool that is built upon a strong core, which contains clearly articulated values and principles that allow for multiple paths to achieving common goals and that scaffolds change and development regardless of the starting point. It promotes a common understanding of ECEC as a multidisciplinary field of practice drawing on theory related to e.g. education, health and family support. The framework creates a language of quality that promotes reflection and which can be adapted to different national, regional and local contexts. The framework proposal carries the potential of being policy driven but at the same time in line with the comprehensive view of quality of ECEC established by researchers.

The question poses itself, however, why put another layer of 'regulation' above the one already existing in the Member States. Why have a European Framework? In this particular context the expert members of the group saw this tool as an efficient means to create the right policy osmosis around the ECEC issue, raise its profile and possibly protect it from budget cuts that it has been threatened by in many Member States.

In practical terms, the framework proposal contains four guiding principles and ten action statements within the five key areas on which policy makers can have direct influence. These are access, workforce, curriculum, evaluation and monitoring, governance and funding. The four guiding principles are the image and voice of a strong competent child who is a partner in learning (research on child development should guide policy work on quality of ECEC); to consider child development as a collaborative project that happens in a coherent, transparent, trusting partnership for better child development; the idea of a competent system that is multi-level and multi-layered and recognises the coherence between policy, research and practice and gears funding towards quality that is evidence based; to focus on process quality which in contrast to structural (Working Group on Early Childhood Education and Care under the auspices of the European Commission, 2014, p. 6.) and outcomes (Working Group on Early Childhood Education and Care under the auspices of the European Commission, 2014, p. 6.) quality focuses on the quality of the relationships and interaction, the sense of identity, belonging, pedagogy and the role of the professional reflective adult. Thus professionalisation of staff is a very important part of the quality concept but is tackled as one part of the whole issue. The glossary of the proposal defined the professional role of staff as 'one which is regulated and requires individuals to develop and reflect on their own practice with parents and children, creating a learning environment which is constantly renewed and improved'. It also emphasises that 'those fulfilling these roles will have appropriate qualifications and will be expected to take responsibility for the provision of high quality ECEC services in line with the available resources and the requirements and expectations of their system' (Proposal, 2014, p. 70). Thus it is essential that the professional role be linked to qualifications and good working conditions, which allow for planning and reflection, and the possibilities of a career path. It is equally important, however, that the professional role fits the particular socio-economic and cultural context in which it is practised.

As set out in the *Proposal for Key Principles of a Quality Framework for ECEC*, high quality ECEC requires:

- provision that is available and affordable to all families and their children;
- provision that encourages participation, strengthens social inclusion and embraces diversity;
- well-qualified staff whose initial and continuing training enables them to fulfil their professional role;
- supportive working conditions, including professional leadership which creates opportunities for observation, reflection, planning, teamwork and cooperation with parents;

- a curriculum based on pedagogic goals, values and approaches which enables children to reach their full potential in a holistic way;
- a curriculum which requires staff to collaborate with children, colleagues and parents and to reflect on their own practice;
- monitoring and evaluating produces information at the relevant local, regional and/or national level to support continuing improvements in the quality of policy and practice;
- monitoring and evaluation, which is in the best interest of the child.

These are easier to achieve if the following governance arrangements are in place:

- Stakeholders in the ECEC system have a clear and shared understanding of their role and responsibilities, and know that they are expected to collaborate with partner organisations;
- Legislation, regulation and/or funding supports progress towards a universal legal entitlement to publicly subsidised or funded ECEC, and progress is regularly reported to all stakeholders.

The statements point to the most important policies, structures and processes that need to be in place so as to deliver high-quality ECEC for all children, which is informed by high expectations. 'High expectations' means that the ECEC system, and staff within the system, is child-centred, creates an environment where children are creatively encouraged to reach their full potential, and that their success and achievement is recognised and seen as an important part of the learning and caring environment. These ten statements when adapted to the local context and taken together can provide a new impetus to ensure the universal availability of high-quality ECEC provision from birth to the start of compulsory primary schooling. The statements are closely linked and interdependent, e.g. increasing access without a guarantee of quality can be detrimental to some children rather than beneficial.

The statements are supported by the latest European evidence base and 20 country examples. These actions are indispensable and interconnected and lead to improvement of quality.

It is important that the evidence base is mainly stemming from European research as at the time of the drafting of the Communication, the international evidence used by policy makers was mainly drawn from English-speaking countries. The Communication and the follow-up Council Conclusions put a great deal of emphasis on widening the European evidence base on ECEC. Since then several studies have been commissioned in the field by interested Directorates General, such as Education and Culture, Employment and Justice as well as within the European 7th Framework Research Programme.

The aim of the framework proposal is to show that care and education in the early years are viewed as inseparable, and the issue of access becomes part of the issue of quality. Child development, and indeed the overall wellbeing of a child, are as significant in a childcare context as in the context of education. Caring for a child to meet their individual needs should not be approached without simultaneously considering their education and vice versa. Some countries have already addressed these issues in a systemic way, and in some other countries there are very good stand-alone initiatives, but the issue is often not addressed right across the system at national level. The initiative should be a useful tool to mainstream accessible, high-quality ECEC across the Member States.

The way forward

There is indeed a growing momentum to reform ECEC policy and provision at European and national levels, and with this there is significant opportunity to make a real difference and real improvements. Mainly connected with recent economic and social challenges discourse there is a policy space for the recognition of the importance of ECEC from the educational perspective. This implies then also the opportunity to make use of the framework proposal on the ground in the Member States.

There are numerous actors present in the ECEC policy scene, from local players to international organisations, NGOs and governmental organisations. It is crucial that there is an active dialogue between all relevant players in order to find the best solutions that are tailor-made for national, regional and local contexts and to serve the best interests of children and their families.

There are several dilemmas concerning the way forward. First, it is important that the field remains loyal to its own values, principles and goals, and that from an educational perspective it does not merely become a preparation for school or in fact a mini-school. Secondly, it also needs to both fit and, at least partly, shape the current policy discourses. Current education policy discourse is overwhelmingly quantitative. So there is a growing tendency in this field, as in all the other policy fields, to rely on the data (preferably of quantitative nature). But in this field there is a lack of comparative quantitative data.

As for the EU's role in this process, there are many who would like the EU to take a stronger role in pushing the agenda forward but some do not wish to see more indicators and benchmarking, which will push for more reporting and 'soft regulation' at European level. And finally, there are actors who simply do not agree with the mainstream quality discourse.

So what can be the next steps in this complex policy space? Apart from coordinating policy co-operation between the European Member States with the Open Method of Coordination, there are a number of other tools through which European level policy making supports national policy making and advances the agreed agenda on creating accessible high-quality ECEC for all children: through the European Union's ten-year strategy for sustainable growth (Europe 2020), through policy debate, through widening the evidence base for policy making and through funding.

The funding programme of the Commission in the field of education and training – Erasmus+ – strongly supports initiatives in the early childhood field, strengthening experimentation and partnerships as well as mainstreaming good practices.

The European Commission emphasises the need for Member States to make efficient use of existing financial tools, such as the different EU funding programmes (and, most importantly, the Structural Funds), which allow for policy experimentation and partnership building as well as research.

Within the European Semester, Member States' progress is monitored and analysed against benchmarks and indicators in all policy sectors. On the basis of this analysis, countries receive country specific recommendations (CSR). These suggest how countries can make policy progress in certain fields. National policies should respond to these CSRs and adjust their investment priorities accordingly. It is interesting to note that in 2013, fourteen countries and in 2014, ten countries received such CSRs specifically concerning their ECEC policy and provision.

Finally, in recent years several studies have been launched by the European Commission, which will broaden the European evidence base concerning ECEC services (Urban et al., 2011; European Commission, 2013b; European Commission, 2014b; 2014c; CARE, forthcoming).

As for further policy development at European level, it would definitely be important to encourage reliable quantitative and qualitative data development and strengthen the relationship between research and policy in the ECEC field. The quality discourse might be a useful tool for that, if it is used as a discursive space which allows for multidisciplinary, multi-level and multi-layered discussion about its meaning and for long-term strategy building with the participation of many interested players.

There is a vast literature on the Europeanisation of the education policy space and on the changing relationship between research and policy. Lately, the tendency has been to identify measurability and quantification as the reliable evidence for policy making. Econometrics is considered the single methodology for measurement, whereas questions regarding the epistemology or ethics of its analyses are never asked (Grek, 2014, p.8.). Moreover, there is a fusion between knowledge and policy, where knowledge is not only there to inform policy but it becomes policy (Neuman, 2012, p. 612). This fusion puts organisations and experts responsible for knowledge production in far more powerful positions. For example, the OECD's education policy work depends, to a significant extent, on stressing the importance of policy factors over the effects of cultural and social contexts. Cultural and historical explanations for the success of education systems cannot be used to justify reform in other nations, whereas pointing to specific policy settings as the cause of success can provide governments with leverage for internal reform agendas (Sellar & Lingard, 2013, p.723). This approach carries, however, the risk that insufficient attention is paid to system-specific factors and contexts. Moreover, interaction between knowledge, power, interest and beliefs are at the heart of governance and thus policy making. This interaction is rather uncharted territory in the research (Fazekas & Burns, 2012, p.23). Consequently, the cultural and social contexts, which also include the way in which knowledge is transferred into policy, need to be retained in the policy discourse. The quality framework proposal on ECEC developed by the working group and the quality discourse itself have the potential to make these factors part of future policy debates on ECEC policies. As a result, EU education policy making in this field carries the potential of taking leadership in this matter. It also promises to counter-balance current trends in education policy making of singling out policy factors at the expense of a disregard for the cultural and social contexts.

It should be clear from the two stories on the dynamic relationship between research and policy in the particular field of ECEC at the European level that to find the best policy solutions in certain points in time for a group of people needs to be based on solid and nuanced qualitative and quantitative evidence and an on-going dialogue between the different players, researchers, practitioners, policy makers and stakeholders at different levels in the system. Moreover, the solution, the policy, should be open for evaluation, and thus revision. The quality debate and the quality framework proposal – including its potential to offer a path for the professionalisation of staff that fits the particular context of ECEC – are very important steps in this direction. If practised well they can carry on truly (re-) connecting the ECEC discourse with current public debates about the democratic establishment, and the design of appropriate education systems that will be suitable for educating citizens across Europe in the future.

Notes

1 *Research* means knowledge production and it needs to go through the hurdle of interpretation, legitimisation by experts (expertise) so that it turns into evidence for policy.
2 *Knowledge* is assimilated information and the understanding of how to use it. Knowledge also contains negotiation, etc. It is not only about scientific knowledge. Often individual experts or expert organisations are involved in knowledge production and knowledge generation.
3 *Governance* refers to a process of governing societies in a situation where no single actor can claim absolute dominance. It is a dynamic process involving implementation, monitoring and decision making.
4 So as to support Member States in the implementation of the targets of the Europe 2020 Strategy that Member States have translated into national targets and growth enhancing policies, the European Commission has set up a yearly cycle of economic policy coordination called the European Semester. Each year the European Commission undertakes a detailed analysis of EU Member States' programmes of economic and structural reforms and provides them with recommendations for the next 12-18 months. For more details see: http://ec.europa.eu/europe2020/making-it-happen/.
5 Provision is measured as children cared for (by formal arrangements other than by the family) as a proportion of all children in the same age group (children under three or between three years and the mandatory school age). This indicator is broken down by the number of hours per week during which the children are cared for (up to 30 hours a week/30 hours or more a week). Data are collected through an EU harmonised survey, the EU Survey on Income and Living Conditions (EU-SILC). Formal arrangements are defined as: organised structure with qualified staff, at a daycare centre or at an organised family daycare.
6 The European benchmark in the Education and Training 2020 strategy is not considered to be a target - as the Barcelona target from 2002 – to be reached by individual countries by 2020. It provides guidance for national policy makers to set national targets or benchmarks in the field.

References

Council Conclusions (2006). *Council Conclusions on efficiency and equity in education and training* (OJ C 298 of 8.12.2006) Retrieved from: http://eur-lex.europa.eu/legal-content/EN/TXT/?uri=CELEX%3A42006X1208(01). Brussels.

Council Conclusions (2008). *Council Conclusions on preparing young people for the 21st century: an agenda for European cooperation on schools* (OJ C 319 of 13.12.2008) Retrieved from: http://eur-lex.europa.eu/legal-content/EN/TXT/?uri=URISERV%3Aef0004. Brussels.

Council Conclusions (2009). *Council Conclusions on a strategic framework for European cooperation in education and training* ('ET2020') (OJ C 119 of 28.5.2009) Retrieved from: http://eur-lex.europa.eu/legal-content/EN/TXT/?uri=uriserv%3Aef0016. Brussels.

Council Conclusions (2011). *Council Conclusions on early childhood education and care: providing all our children with the best start for the world of tomorrow*, 2011/C 175/03. Retrieved from: http://eur-lex.europa.eu/legal-content/EN/TXT/PDF/?uri=CELEX:52011XG0615(04)&from=EN. Brussels.

Council Recommendation (1992). *Council Recommendation 92/241/EEC of 31 March 1992 on Childcare*, OJ [1992] L 123. Retrieved from: http://eur-lex.europa.eu/legal-content/EN/TXT/PDF/?uri=CELEX:31992H0241&from=EN. Brussels.

European Commission (2006). *Roadmap for Equality between Women and Men (2006–2010)*, SEC (2006) 275. Brussels: European Commission. Retrieved from: http://eur-lex.europa.eu/legal-content/EN/TXT/PDF/?uri=CELEX:52006DC0092&from=EN. Brussels: European Commission.

European Commission (2008). Implementation of the Barcelona objectives concerning childcare facilities for pre-school aged children, COM (2008) 598; SEC (2008) 2524. Brussels: European Commission.

European Commission (2011). Communication from the European Commission: Early Childhood Education and Care – providing all children with the best start for the world of tomorrow, COM (2011) 66 final. Retrieved from: http://eur-lex.europa.eu/legal-content/EN/TXT/PDF/?uri=CELEX:52011DC0066&from=EN.

European Commission (2013a). Barcelona objectives: the development of childcare facilities for young children in Europe with a view to sustainable and inclusive growth. Brussels: European Commission.

European Commission (2013b). Study on the effect on ECEC on inclusion: ECEC for children from disadvantaged backgrounds – findings from a European literature review and two case studies. Brussels: European Commission.

European Commission (2014a). Education Monitor. Brussels: European Commission.

European Commission (2014b). Study on the effective use of early childhood education and care in preventing early school leaving. Brussels: European Commission.

European Commission (2014c). A study on conditional cash transfers (CCTs) and their impact on children. Brussels: European Commission.

European Parliament (2002). Presidency conclusions: Barcelona European Council – 16 March 2002. Brussels: European Parliament and Council.

Fazekas, M. & Burns, T. (2012). Exploring the complex interaction between governance and knowledge in education, *OECD Education Working Papers*, 67. Paris: OECD Publishing. DOI: 10.1787/19939019.

Grek, S. (2014). OECD as a site of coproduction: European education governance and the new politics of 'policy mobilisation', *Critical Policy Studies*, 8(3), 266–281.

Gromley Jr & William T. (2011). From science to policy in early childhood. *Science*, 333, 978–981.

NESSE (2009). *Early childhood education and care: key lessons from research for policy makers*. Brussels: NESSE.

Neuman, E. (2012). Quantifying quality: the construction of Europe and the road to policy learning, *European Educational Research Journal*, 11(4), 609–615.

Ozga, J., Dahler-Larsen, P., Segerholm, Ch. & Simola, H. (Eds.) (2011). *Fabricating quality in education: data and governance in Europe*. Abingdon: Routledge.

Sellar, S. & Lingard, B. (2013). The OECD on global governance in education, *Journal of Education Policy*, 28(5), 710–725.

Urban, M., Vandenbroeck, M., Lazzari, A., Peeters, J., & Van Laere, K. (2011). *Competence requirements for early childhood education and care*. London and Ghent: UEL and UGent.

Working Group on Early Childhood Education and Care under the auspices of the European Commission (2014). Proposal for Key Principles for a Quality Framework in ECEC. Retrieved from: http://ec.europa.eu/education/policy/strategic-framework/archive/documents/ecec-quality-framework_en.pdf.

9

LESSONS LEARNT AND A DEBATE TO BE CONTINUED

Jan Peeters, Mathias Urban and Michel Vandenbroeck

At the time of writing this book six years have passed since we finalised *Competence Requirements in Early Childhood Education and Care* (CoRe), a study commissioned by the European Commission, DG Education and Culture (Urban et al., 2011). The study was based on a literature review, a survey in 15 EU countries and a series of in-depth case studies. For this book, these case studies have been revised and updated by their original authors. They provide unique insights into experiences that are not commonly made visible in the international literature in our field – which remains dominated by English as its medium and by experiences and narratives from an English language (US, UK) context. Taken together, the case studies not only show the diversity of possible pathways to develop professionalism in a wide range of early childhood contexts, they also open deeper understandings of how to develop *competent systems* – a concept that was central in the conclusions of the CoRe study.

At the level of the individual practitioner, the English case study shows how the appetite for learning in practice and for continuous professional development (CPD) can be enhanced and it illustrates the relevance of open-minded, proactive teachers. The Danish pre-service training is an interesting example of how personal and academic reflections go hand in hand and are maintained in a delicate balance. Daily practice as a basis for learning and for theorising through shared reflection is key to the experiences of the professionalisation policies of the cities of Pistoia and Ghent and it characterises the approach taken by ESSE (*École Santé Social Sud-Est*) in Lyon, where practitioners with low formal qualifications are educated to bachelor level. The Lyon case sheds light on the complexity behind increasing the levels of qualification, as it illustrates how enhancing individual competences through 'training' can create tensions in the team. Teams need to develop the necessary competences to deal with the changes in professional identity of those who combine work and training. The case studies of Ghent and Pistoia also show how this relates to competences at the institutional level. The characteristics of the municipal institutions in these two cities enable close collaboration between professionals with different status, and the continuous and reciprocal exchange between professionals and parents from diverse backgrounds. These exchanges result in a common culture and a shared understanding of what is desirable for children, as well as in shared ethical values. A similar key lesson can be drawn from the Slovenian case study, where this common culture has been cherished, despite differences in the professional status of practitioners. The Slovenian and the Ghent case studies also show that working in a context of diversity can increase professional reflexivity, provided the teams can benefit from coaching and inspired leadership.

On the broader scale of interagency collaboration and local governments, the Danish case shows how initial training, working conditions and recruitment are intertwined. Although the Danish early childhood education and care (ECEC) system has a universal coverage (including children under the age of three) the Danish ECEC sector does not experience the shortages of staff or problems of recruitment that dominate the sector in other EU Member States. This is due to the high status of the profession of 'pedagogue' and the comparatively high salaries (compared to other countries). The Danish case also provides an example of a common culture and a shared image of the child, an image of an active and competent child that is shared by the colleges, practitioners and the local authorities. This broad interpretation of professionalism in ECEC – characterised by particular attention for the inclusion of culture, nature and aesthetic forms of expression in the initial professional preparation – is probably one of the reasons why there are more male students and male educators compared to other countries.

The key role of competent governance is made clear in several of the case studies presented in this book. Legislations differ substantially across Europe. This is illustrated, for instance, by the fact that in England many different qualifications co-exist, while the Danish ECEC services have one general qualification. While the Flemish preschool teachers have parity of pay, compared to primary and secondary school teachers, this is not the case in several other cases presented here. Despite these differences, it is clear that structural conditions (and thus competent governance) are necessary, including decent working conditions, child-free hours for continuous professional development, adequate funding, etc. In all these aspects, the case studies reiterate and deepen different aspects of the *competent system* that is emphasised by the CoRe study. In particular, the Polish case on the WTANT programme eloquently talks about how all these competence levels are interrelated, and how problems at one level impact on other levels. The Polish programme also shows how grassroots organisations can successfully challenge the governance of an education system that is overregulated and teacher-oriented towards mainstream educational institutions.

All case studies bring the analysis forward and have also begun to explore a next level: the international one. Several of the practices described here have benefited from international exchange, thanks to European exchange programmes. There have been peer visits of trainers and practitioners between Pistoia and Ghent, and between Ghent and Lyon, for instance. But, crucially, the chapter by Nóra Milotay also shows how the international level can substantially contribute to competent systems. Whilst ECEC is subject of the principle of subsidiarity, the European Quality Framework on ECEC, which was developed through the Open Method of Coordination, is an interesting example of the important role international organisations can play in promoting quality in ECEC. It is a document that is embedded in research, yet it is also a political document, which has the support of a broad network of stakeholders and policy makers.

Despite all these achievements, it is clear that many challenges remain. Europe is facing an economic downturn and widespread austerity measures (cuts to public budgets) impact on working conditions as well as on Member States' investment in initial professional preparation and CPD. Increasingly, the European project seems to accept rising levels of inequality as inevitable, with some countries officially abandoning child poverty targets. The increase in numbers of incoming refugees has unveiled a worrying lack of solidarity between European countries – a fundamental principle of the EU has proven to be dysfunctional. And while Europe keeps building fences (Calais, Hungary) against refugees, growing up under conditions of abject poverty has become a common experience for an increasing number of children from marginalised groups in Europe – most notably Roma and Traveller.

In such times, policy makers may be tempted to concentrate on short-term solutions, while we now know that a long-term vision on ECEC is crucial, as the English case study has illustrated. Sustained investments are necessary, considering the high numbers of unqualified assistant staff in many EU countries. In addition, it is beyond doubt that the diversity of the populations of young children will further increase across Europe. *Competent systems* that are able to deal with diversity, complexity and unpredictability are needed more than ever. In these contexts of increasing diversity (both ethnic and socio-economic) and inequality, it is important to maintain a focus on equal opportunities, equal conditions and more just and equal outcomes (the latter being conspicuously absent from the mainstream early childhood policy debate in Europe). A further challenge is that European approaches to early childhood education and care are based on a rather limited understanding of the integration of *childcare* and *early education* as inseparable complements. Within this integration, *care* is too often seen as a function to support learning and early education (Van Laere, Peeters, & Vandenbroeck, 2012). There is still a long road ahead towards a deeper understanding and recognition of the value of care as a fundamental aspect of human society and of democracy (Tronto, 2013). These are challenges that cannot be resolved by isolated and short-term initatives, as these have only a limited impact on daily practice, if any. They require sustained efforts on all levels instead.

The CoRe data and the case studies presented in this book provide a solid evidence base for our key argument: that professional *competence* cannot be sufficiently understood as a characteristic of the individual practitioner (teacher, educator, childcare worker). Instead, *competence* unfolds in reciprocal relationships between all elements of the early childhood *system*: individuals, institutions, and the governance of the system on national and even on international levels. It is therefore futile (and unsustainable) to concentrate efforts and scarce resources on only one aspect of that system. Our best (and only, as we argue) chance to change practices in order to achieve better, more equitable outcomes for all children and families is to address all elements simultaneously, focusing (and resourcing) the relationships *between* them.

The principle of systemic approaches, highlighted in CoRe, has been received favourably in the European Union policy context. The 2011 EU Communication on 'Early Childhood Education and Care' (European Commission, 2011) explicitly states that systemic approaches to professionalising the early childhood field are needed; this message is endorsed by Member States (Council of the European Union, 2011). The recognition of the *competent system* approach at EU level is mirrored at national and local level across Europe. BKK, the Dutch '*Quality Bureau child care centres*' responsible for taking initiatives to increase the quality of the childcare services in the Netherlands was inspired by CoRe; it has set up 11 pilot projects to develop competent systems in childcare organisations (Boonstra & Jepma, 2014). At local level, to give just one example, the City of Utrecht, the Netherlands, has drawn on the CoRe principles to rewrite its municipal Quality Framework for childcare services (City of Utrecht, 2013). On a larger scale, a major player in the German early childhood context, the Bertelsmann Foundation, is adopting the concept of *competent systems* as its key strategy to promote reform of the early childhood system across Germany's federal structure and is currently funding an international research project to extend the original CoRe project beyond the EU. Countries like Ireland are beginning to recognise the need for a systemic approach to reforming their desperately fragmented early childhood system.

In the Flemish Community of Belgium, the recommendations of the CoRe project have influenced new legislation on childcare, indeed the new law states that every person who works with young children (from birth to three) must be supported by a pedagogical coach. To implement this new law, a large-scale project on coaching was set up within independent childcare centres (Vlaamse Regering, 2012).

The need to *professionalise* the early childhood workforce has long been at the centre of the discussion about forming and reforming early childhood services in Europe and internationally. With it came an often-controversial debate about concepts and understandings of *professionalism* in early childhood. Over the years the authors of this book and many others have contributed to this debate, arguing that professionalism in early childhood care and education cannot be understood with mere traditional structural-functionalist, managerial or technocratic concepts (Miller, Dalli & Urban, 2012; Oberhümer, 2005; Oberhümer, Schreyer & Neuman, 2010; Oberhümer & Ulich, 1997; Peeters, 2008; Urban, 2008). Local organisations, but also international networks like DECET (www.decet.org) and ISSA (www.issa.nl) have brought together researchers and practitioners to redefine professionalism to promote social justice, diversity and equality for all children and adults in early childhood. The CoRe project, including the case studies presented in this book, has extended this thinking about what it means to be professional in early childhood into the wider context of the early childhood policy and practice

system. All of this was – and continues to be – crucial for the development of practice and academic discipline in our field.

References

Boonstra, M. & Jepma I. (2014). *Lerenderwijs. Samen werken aan pedagogische kwaliteit in de
kinderopvang*. Amsterdam: Reed Business Education.

City of Utrecht. (2013). *Utrechts kwaliteitskader voor educatie van het jonge kind. Aanbevelingen
voor versterking van professionele competenties voor medewerkers, team en organisatie*. Utrecht:
Utrechtse Onderwijsagenda.

Council of the European Union. (2011). *Council conclusions of 15 June 2011 on early childhood
education and care: providing all our children with the best start for the world of tomorrow*. Brussels:
Official Journal of the European Union.

European Commission. (2011). *Early childhood education and care: providing all our children with
the best start for the world of tomorrow*. Brussels: European Commission, Directorate General
for Education and Culture.

Miller, L., Dalli, C. & Urban, M. (Eds.). (2012). *Early childhood grows up: towards a critical
ecology of the profession*. Dordrecht and London: Springer.

Oberhümer, P. (2005). Conceptualising the Early Childhood Pedagogue: Policy Approaches
and Issues of Professionalism. *European Early Childhood Education Research Journal, 13*(1),
5–16.

Oberhümer, P, Schreyer, I. & Neuman, M. J. (2010). *Professionals in early childhood education
and care systems: European profiles and perspectives*. Opladen and Farmington Hills: Barbara
Budrich Publishers.

Oberhümer, P. & Ulich, M. (1997). *Working with young children in Europe: provision and staff
training*. London: Paul Chapman.

Peeters, J. (2008). *The construction of a new profession: a European perspective on professionalism in
early childhood education and care*. Amsterdam: SWP Publishers.

Tronto, J.C. (2013). *Caring democracy: markets, equality and justice*. New York and London:
New York University Press.

Urban, M., Vandenbroeck, M., Lazzari, A., Peeters, J. & Van Laere, K. (2011). *Competence
requirements for early childhood education and care*. London and Ghent: UEL and UGent.

Urban, M. (2008). Dealing with Uncertainty: Challenges and Possibilities for the Early
Childhood Profession. *European Early Childhood Education Research Journal, 16*(2),
135–152.

Van Laere, K., Peeters, J. & Vandenbroeck, M. (2012). The Education and Care Divide:
The Role of the Early Childhood Workforce in 15 European Countries. *European
Journal of Education, 47*(4), 527–541.

Vlaamse Regering. (2012) *Decreet kinderopvang van baby's en peuters van 20 april 2012*.
Brussels: Vlaamse Regering.

INDEX